Brian Lamont was born in
school at 15 and worked in a variety of jobs that include labourer, gardener, pest exterminator, graphics assistant, bowling green attendant, dishwasher, boiler man, electrician's mate and office clerk. In 1995, following an Access course at the Centre for Continuing Education in Edinburgh, he entered Edinburgh University where he graduated with a MA Honours degree in English literature.

FIRST IMPRESSIONS

Brian Lamont

Penbury Press, 2005

First Impressions
ISBN 0-9548789-0-6

Published by:
Penbury Press
PO Box 28268
Edinburgh
EH9 1ZL
E-mail: penburypress@yahoo.co.uk
Web-site: http://penburypress.blogspot.com

Design & production co-ordinated by:
The ***Better Book*** Company Ltd
Havant
Hampshire
PO9 2XH

Printed in England

To Dave Thain

(fact stranger than fiction)

Look how we can, or sad, or merrily,
Interpretation will misquote our looks.
William Shakespeare, *Henry IV, Pt I* (1598)

Every one knew how laborious the usual method is of attaining to the arts and sciences; whereas by his contrivance the most ignorant person at a reasonable charge, and with a little bodily labour, may write books in philosophy, poetry, politics, law, mathematics, and theology, without the least assistance from genius or study.
Jonathan Swift, *Gulliver's Travels* (1726)

Eeyore was saying to himself, 'This writing business. Pencils and what-not. Over-rated, if you ask me. Silly stuff. Nothing in it.' A.A. Milne, *Winnie-the-Pooh* (1926)

Contents

Acknowledgements

With all thanks possible to my family, friends and teachers.

Particular thanks to Carol for her practical advice and unwavering support, and to Andrew who can always be relied on for an encouraging 'Well, it's not bad I suppose' (which is high praise indeed).

Thanks also to Hellen, to George, to Kirsty, to Niki, to Ann, to Fiona, to Luca and Collette, and to Denise, all of whom were subjected to the idea.

Special thanks to Gilbert for supplying the Margery Allingham novels, to Alan and to Adie for advising on the software, and to the staff of Edinburgh public libraries.

Finally, this book would not have been possible without the assistance and previous work of Mr Norman Macleod and Prof. H.G. Widdowson, upon whose shoulders the author merely stood.

Introduction

> If thou beest more, thou art an understander, and then I trust thee.
>
> Ben Jonson, 'To the Reader'
> *The Alchemist* (1612)

I wasn't going to bother with this bit – it's an afterthought.

Chronologically speaking, if that's at all possible, it should really appear at the end because it was the last thing I wrote, and there are people who say introductions should always be written last because by then you've got a pretty good idea about what it is you want to say. But an introduction at the end of a book would just be stupid, so it's here, at the beginning, instead.

Actually, to be perfectly honest with you, I'm having a bit of difficulty writing this, so I'm just going to waffle on for a while until something appropriate springs to mind... but now several hours have gone by since I began and I'm still not entirely sure where it's all leading.

What do you think of the quotation above? It's pretty impressive sitting up there at the top of the page like that, wouldn't you agree? Adds to the whole... what have you. Very intellectual if you ask me. I also think it's rather clever. I'm not sure why I think it's clever, it just looks clever. It looks as if the person who wrote it knew exactly what they were talking about and was about to say something really interesting. Well, it's probably not a very good example because he really did know what he was talking about and he does go on to say something really interesting, but the point I was trying to make was... all I'm really trying to say is... well, you'll work it out. Brian Lamont (Jun. 2004)

Sign Language

(a sort of 'Preface')

The future could bring many opportunities to make new friends, broaden your horizons and even change the way you view the world around you. As a result, you may experience feelings of uncertainty, confusion and even bewilderment at times. Try not to get disheartened or frustrated. Gradually you will overcome these feelings as you begin to recognise your own achievements.

If you are presented with unfamiliar issues or difficult questions, follow your instincts but make sure emotions alone don't rule your decisions. Persistence will be rewarded and viewing problems as a challenge should develop your confidence.

Love

You could give a partner cause for concern over trivial matters, but if you are really meant for each other, these problems will resolve themselves and only bring you closer together.

A chance encounter could find you hopelessly attracted to someone who seems the perfect match, or perhaps you may look at an old acquaintance in a different light. Remember: appearances can be deceptive.

Money

You may not acquire as much money as you'd like, but recent expenditure should prove beneficial.

Health

Emotional health and personal growth are your prime objectives. Take regular exercise and keep active, but don't forget to find time to relax.

Perhaps you'll undertake a hobby or course of study and cram more into your busy schedule. If you suffer from stress, don't take on too much or attempt to do everything at once; it is important to pace yourself if you are to stay healthy.

You may feel under pressure to conform with others by what you read about in books and magazines. If so, why not try losing a little bit of weight?

Should you wish to give up cigarettes or the excessive use of alcohol and drugs, now could be the best time to start.

Career

Make the most of your talents, and don't be afraid to push yourself more than you normally would – you may discover gifts you never knew you had.

Travel

Throw caution to the wind and get away from it all for a few days, although bear in mind that foreign holidays and weekend excursions usually require planning.

Home and Family

Communication is a marvellous thing, so why not share your experiences with others instead of keeping them all to yourself? The occasional discussion among family and friends will also help relieve tension and prevent future confrontations.

Home life may distract you from an important project or pursuit of interest. Make sure you set aside enough time for these priorities, but avoid work or leisure activities interfering with domestic commitments.

Don't be afraid to ask for assistance if things are troubling you or getting out of hand. You could find encouragement and support from those around you.

Be honest with others, but most importantly with yourself.

Purple and 37 for luck.

Wasted Talent

in respect of...

> a people that jeoparded their lives unto the death in the high places of the field. *Judges* 5:18

During the early years of the 20th century, a series of anonymous rhymes appeared in several modest publications throughout the south-east counties of England that depict a unique rural landscape, propagated by a host of colourful characters. They are rustic poems that celebrate, in tuneful verse, the working lives and simple pleasures of country folk, often within an idyllic and perhaps even artificial environment. These *Country Capers*, as they came to be known, are found in printed material of the period as diverse as local newspapers, political pamphlets, religious treatise and even commercial advertisements. Like the honest, hardworking and fiercely religious people they describe, who seem impervious to circumstance, they are traditionally vicarious, informal and unassuming, and always end on a note of cheerful optimism.

Although never widely distributed, possibly due to the often bawdy nature of their subject, as in 'The Holiday Hoe' (1907) and 'Fanny's Furrow' (1909), the content of which would certainly have offended the delicate sensibilities of mainstream Edwardian society, the verses proved extremely popular within the provinces and created much speculation about their origin.

In an essay entitled 'Static Stanzas', the respected theologian and literary critic Quentin Muse expands on the view expressed in his extensive and, some would say, 'definitive study of southern English folklore, music and poetry' (*Tomes Today*, Jan. 2001), and maintains his previous argument that 'these things [the poems] are most certainly the collective effort of several hands exploiting the success of the form' (*Pastoral Pleasures*, 1999). Furthermore, for Muse, 'their intrinsic value as historic and regional commentary must surely diminish in the absence of authentic attribution' (*Yesteryear's Poets*, Oct. 2001).

The miscellaneous tone of the collection, some 27 completed poems in all, does seem to support this view, with 'Arcadian Dawn' (1906) as perhaps the most incongruous. For instance, lines 12 and 13 vehemently maintain:

> Upon this land for we alone to view,
> When in our nation lie the chosen few.

This is obviously a marked departure from 'And in His eyes all souls will shine,/While mindful of the earth as Thine', as in 'To Chapel' (1906).

The ambiguity of these lines is no less controversial, although their literal meaning appears to lean more favourably towards the indolence of absentee landlords and the indifference of squires and stewards to the hardship of their tenants, rather than, as has been suggested throughout the last century, to any affiliation with numerous religious groups, British political parties, both left and rightwing extremists and, most recently, white supremacists. In his personal and far-reaching diatribe 'From Adam to Adolf' (May, 2004), Rufus T. Hinklebottom draws widely from both popular and classical sources, and regards these sentiments as 'a single comparable voice proclaiming the imminent resurgence of the Aryan race' (*www.sensitivenazis.org*). Of the work as a whole Hinklebottom also favours the mass authorship theory, however, in the villages, towns and Shires of their conception, by people who still maintain a genuine and resolute affection for the poems, they are commonly believed to be the work of one man.

Edwin Boles was a remarkable talent by all accounts. He was born on Christmas Day, 1884, in the village of Lower Hawthorn in Norfolk, where his father owned a small general store. His mother Sarah came from Tamley in Lancashire and worked in the cotton industry, until she reportedly 'fled the county following the disappearance of 65l. 7s. 9d. from the counting room of Throttle's Mill on the evening of Thursday the 17th' (*Blackburn Gazette*, Aug. 19, 1882). Sarah suffered from repeated bouts of pleurisy and influenza, but the southern air and country life seem to have suited her as frequent requisites from the Hawthorn Apothecary, meticulously recorded by the then proprietor Abel S. Gibbons, gradually diminish from their peak on her arrival in the village in October 1882. Sarah must have been welcomed in her new home and was married on April 7, 1883. However, 11 months later, following 'complications in labour from which she never recovered' (Dr Ezra Wisbeach, *Journal*, Jan. 4, 1884), she died at the age of 17 leaving Edwin her only child.

On the afternoon of July 8, 1956, Jonathan Mainwaring, a radio producer for the BBC, received a urgent telegram at his home in Croydon from Tobias J. Sedgwick reading 'Boils require treatment STOP Unable to attend STOP'.

Prof. Sedgwick of Imperial College, the University of London, was billed to appear on the very popular Sunday night programme *Science Made Simple*, in which 'a guest speaker from the scientific community would give an informative talk on his chosen profession and answer listeners' questions' (*Radio Guide*, Jul. 7-13, 1956). The evening's programme was eventually presented by Fred Adcock, who was introduced as '"a recognised authority on the development of farming tools, trades and technology". Ha!' (Henrietta Grant, *Letter to Stephen Embleton, Regional Chairman, PQES, Finchley*, Jul. 9, 1956). No recording of the broadcast survives, but the event was marked by a flood of letters pleading for the return of Mr Adcock, who subsequently appeared in a series of programmes called *A Morsel o' Victuals*, which ran for six consecutive weeks throughout that summer.

Mr Adcock had moved to London from Norfolk in December the previous year and, 'before acquiring his new found fame on the wireless, had supported himself as a domestic gardener in the Croydon area and was practically a vagrant' (Henrietta Grant, *Letter to Lady Hillary Carmichael, President PQES*, Jul. 15, 1956). The programmes proved a great success and a written transcript of each was made by Miss Henrietta Grant, Mr Mainwaring's personal secretary. However, either due to the Corporation's then dispassionate attitude towards British dialects and regional accents, or perhaps Miss Grant's entrenched principals as an active member of the Preservation of the Queen's English Society, the documents in question resonate nothing of what one listener describes as 'Mr Adcock's aberrant and unintelligible drone that washes over the ears like a damp flannel and has no place in a civilized home' (Lady Hillary Carmichael, 'Letter to The Editor', *Radio Guide*, Jul. 21-27, 1956).

Nevertheless, an interesting passage from 'Programme Two' of the series finds Adcock recalling events from his childhood in the village of Lower Hawthorn – and a boy he remembers there named 'Eddy'.

> We (were) Church, you see? He (was) Chapel. Methodist, (yes). That whole side (was) Methodist. Funny people, Methodists. Pleasant enough, I s(up)pose but... Mostly thought they (were) a step above us, they did. Highly, what's the word? Superior, that's it! Highly superior they used to think they (were) – to the likes (of) us. (Yes), you could always tell Chapel folk.
>
> Eddy (was) one (of) that brigade. Eddy... someth(ing) or other, I forget now. Strange lad, Eddy. A real (???), as we used to call them. Always on his own... convers(ing) with God

knows what, I don't know – thin air most (of) the time I reckon. A deep one, Eddy.

Once, spring it (was), we boys, the Hawthorn Rascals as we (were) known, stumbled upon him one morn(ing) afore school. I can see him now, (foolish boy), sitt(ing) under a silver birch tree on the moss covered banks (of) a secluded pond behind old Mr Wakefield's barn, the sun in his face and his head in the (blessed) clouds, while the mayflies danced about his boots. (Splendid) pair (of) boots, we thought.

(*Pauses*)

In (those) days, listeners, you (have) to remember every village had a squire, and every squire had a wayward son – and our village (was) no exception. Squire Gravitt (was) his name and the lad in question (was) Hadley – Hadley Gravitt. Big strapp(ing) bloke, he (was), a great (swell at parties), lord (of) the harvest and a regular patron (of) the Hawthorn Inn. Now, to the north (of) the village (was) a broken down cottage deep in the middle (of) Bracket's Wood, where there lived an old hermit who, they say, had been a cavalry officer dur(ing) the Crimean War and lost both his feet at the Battle (of) Balaclava. We boys used to call him 'Peggy', as he'd hobble about on two wooden stumps on the end (of) his legs and could never catch you over soft ground. For that reason all the grown-ups called him 'Good-to-Firm', but to we boys he (was) just plain 'Peggy'. 'Peggy' never went near the village and no one ever went near 'Peggy', except a young simple girl called Jess Clayton, who worked as a chambermaid up at the manor and visited the old chap every Sunday.

One morn(ing), middle (of) winter it (was), if I recall, old Mr Wakefield found Jess drowned in the pond behind his barn, and when Dr Wisbeach (was) called he confirmed the rumours she'd been expect(ing). Jess had never mentioned (her condition) to anyone, nor (was) it certain who the father (was), but everyone knew he (was) the squire's son.

That day at school the talk (was of) noth(ing) else, and young Samuel Dobson (was) obliged to break his cane over Ted Cocker's (backside) for continuous chatter. While he (was) out (of) the room fetch(ing) another, we boys, as we often did, had a quick tug at his desk drawer, which he always kept locked, and again we (were resigned to disappointment). Well, (imagine our surprise) when that part (of) the desk shot open and its contents fell upon the floor. What (forbidden and corrupting material could our esteemed headmaster possibly wish to conceal from his adoring class?) Noth(ing), it seemed to us, except a well-thumbed copy (of) *Mrs Warburton's Parlour*, *The Complete Works (of) William Shakespeare*, a tiny bottle (of) white powder and a short length (of) rubber hose. Fred Tolley took one sniff (of) the white powder and spent the rest (of) the year eat(ing) chalk. Jake Gourlay played a swift verse (of) 'Onward Christian Soldiers' on the hose. Tom Adams searched in vain for a picture (of) Mrs Warburton, while (Tubby Plumb and I) looked for (rude words) in the great man's work. We (were) all so busy laugh(ing) no one noticed Mr Dobson fum(ing) at the door, and when he (came) in he walloped the lot (of) us.

That even(ing) we (were) in Proctor's Meadow try(ing) to remember what we'd read. Young Eddy (was) in the mixed infants so he'd missed all the excitement, but when he heard (those) words he recognised them immediately. 'Lucrece', it (was, very colourful too) as I understand, and he knew it backwards. So, what we did (was), we got him to write us down a portion in return for his boots, and we pinned it up on the church notice board. Then we wrote 'G.T.F.' on the bottom so all the grown-ups would think it (was) the work (of) old 'Peggy' tak(ing) a stab at the village.

Well, (would you believe it)? That bit (of) paper stayed up there for nearly a week. No one touched it, not a soul, not even the Rev. John who walked passed it two or three times a day and put other things up alongside. There it (was) for all the world to see – and no one said a word.

(*Pauses*)

The follow(ing) Saturday the Hawthorn Rascals (were) in Mire's Lane when who should hobble along but old 'Peggy' under a great bundle (of) firewood. We all began gather(ing) up clods (of) earth, and just as we (were) about to (make his life a misery) young Hadley Gravitt (came) thunder(ing) down the lane on Hellfire. The old man didn't move a muscle and as the great horse thundered past Hadley Gravitt thrashed him across the mouth with his rid(ing) whip. We all bolted for the woods in terror, but shortly after I popped my head out to see if the coast (was) clear and what do you s(up)pose? There (was) young Eddy help(ing) the old man out (of) the (mud) and back onto his stumps.

That afternoon they held the service for Jess Clayton. I heard Dan Tamworth at the harmonium play(ing) 'At Even, Ere the Sun (was) Set', and it seemed the whole village had turned out to send her off.

The next morn(ing) I took a walk over to the churchyard to see the grave. She (was) buried under a simple wooden cross beside an empty plot on one side and her mother on the other. I can still remember the words on that stone. 'Mary Anne Clayton', it said. 'Born 1848, died 1883. Mother (of) Jessy, beloved wife (of) Lieutenant Henry John Clayton, killed in action, Transvaal 1881, daughter (of) Major Granville Thomas Fletcher'.

(*Pauses*)

I never called him 'Peggy' again after that.

In the spring of 1896, the village of Lower Hawthorn was struck by a great hurricane that 'swept across the county leaving a trail of devastation in its wake' (Dr Ezra Wisbeach, *Journal*, Mar. 24, 1896). The storm was confined to the south-west and higher ground, but 'several homes and businesses were destroyed including Boles' Provisions, the Hawthorn Inn and the Manor, which took a direct hit' (*ibid*). Intriguingly, Dr Wisbeach further reports that immediately following the event:

> The entire populace was dumbfounded and languished among a disquieting silence that had settled upon the village. Suddenly a commotion broke forth, and down the road came the squire's horse in a frantic condition before it struck the water trough and was rendered unconscious. The beast had two broken hooves and has since been destroyed, but as yet there is no sign of the rider. I can only hope that not more calamity has befallen this unfortunate family of late.

The storm proved a significant turning point, and Edwin Boles moved to the market town of Mude where he lived with his great-aunt Cecilia, while his father disappeared for several years without trace. Cecilia Boles was an elderly spinster, a tireless evangelical and a virulent exponent of the temperance movement. As an avid subscriber to *The Joyous Season*, a quarterly publication for 'good-living Christians' that lists the forthcoming sermons of preachers throughout the county, she apparently thought nothing of travelling up to 30 miles in a day to hear her favourites. Miss Boles also kept a comprehensive register of preachers on the circuit and detailed the many services that she attended. These include those of such notable characters as the famous Noah Gass of East Harling, 'marvellous diction', Ichobod Winswimsy of Thetford, 'splendid posture', and the great Josiah Stains of Garboldishham, who is listed as simply 'Outstanding!'

Although it is reasonable to assume that Cecelia Boles was accompanied by her great-nephew on these occasions, what effect this highly personal and usually self-expressionist form of worship had on the young Edwin must surely remain conjecture.

Edwin's formal education, however, having 'exasperated' his elementary teacher 'to the point of distraction' (Elizabeth Dobson, *Letter to Isaiah Boles*, Mar. 27, 1892), is said to have been 'exemplary but only when in attendance, which is rare, and his mind attentive to his studies, which is even rarer' (Mude Grammar, *Records*, 1898-9).

The school provided for the children of better-off trades people, shopkeepers and farmers but apparently 'failed to recognise the obvious ability of a local boy who had committed in its entirety the New Testament to memory by the age of nine and is presently working upon the Old' (Rev. Samuel Theaks, *Diary*, May 12, 1895).

On leaving school Boles was employed by S. Wheeler & Co., 'purveyors of quality remnants, ribbons and haberdashery' (*Handbill*, *c.* 1900), and he remained there until the death of Cecelia Boles in July 1904. In the same year Boles left his great-aunt's house and became a lay preacher, travelling widely throughout southern England and taking occasional work to sustain his ministerial calling, but he never settled in one place more than a few weeks before moving on.

Boles was not particular about where he preached, and his name is found in documents across the region as much among Anglicans, Baptists, Congregationalists and even the Salvation Army, as it is within the ranks of his own Methodist community. Working alongside farmhands, labourers and ditch-diggers while spreading the gospel was a period of Bole's life he probably enjoyed, and it also coincides with the capers at their most prolific. Boles' sermons were renowned and he became something of a minor celebrity, described as:

> ... one who, on the Lord's Day, can fill our dear church to bursting with souls from far and wide, both high and low, who arrive from daybreak on to sit in patient anticipation of this wondrous spirit, heaven-sent with the voice of God.
>
> St Jude's, Millthorp, *Parish Magazine* (Apr. 1909)

In 1913, through the advice and influence of the Rev. Spokes at Thosby in Suffolk, Boles entered Cambridge where he read theology and classics, but abandoned his studies the following year. A fellow student recalls 'a tall ungainly figure, always solitary, who never attended lectures nor made any concerted effort to engage with others or university life (E.S. Potts, *My Personal Studies in Selfish Behaviour*,

1929). Yet Boles is said to have been 'a great orator', and private readings of his religious verse are fondly remembered in the autobiography of Cyril Shroud, with whom a brief friendship transpired, as 'pure illuminations of faith' (*Dreaming Inspires*, 1946). Shroud, who left Cambridge in 1914 having secured a position at Oxford where he later became professor of philosophy, says of Boles:

> He had the most powerful presence that I have ever encountered in any man, and possessed an abundance of good charm and dignity. While he insisted that we must all follow our path in life, should it cross or part with another, I was sorry to leave him. I must sadly confirm that I never saw him again.

Apart from a few disputed notebooks held by the Coroner's Office in Mude, there is no evidence of the work to which Shroud refers, nor any indication of what it was that so distracted Boles from his studies. The poems that exist may seem trivial in comparison to that which is lost and can only be imagined, yet the personal nature of the verse suggests that it was never intended for public consumption. What remains, however, is a vibrant collection of melodic, vivacious and merry broad-jestings that capture the sights and sounds of an age of innocence, when the world seemed a simple and safer place in which to live – and it was summer all year round.

On the Road to Applegate Farm

Big hefty men wi' picks an' shovels,
Huge lumps o' lad wi' scythe an' rake,
Met at crossin' (sure o' trouble),
Watched by girls from Applegate.

Sleeves wor rolled an' hands a-spatted,
Boots an' fists wor most irate,
Blood wi' teeth in dust wor splattered,
All for maids o' Applegate.

Dazed an' smartin', wheezin', coughin',
Shattered blokes bereft o' hate,
Keelin', kneelin', lyin', laughin' -
Lost wor girls from Applegate.

Peace restored an' none the victor,
Cider beckons fond embrace.
Best o' chums, no thoughts to wrestlin',
Least wi' girls o' Applegate. (1910)

Boles, perhaps disillusioned by academic life, returned to his native county and preaching, although now, at a time of national emergency, religious gatherings were often combined with compelling demands for military registration. Boles answered the call himself on May 1, 1915, and served as an officer with the 7th (Service) Battalion of the Royal Norfolk Regiment. In the chaos and confusion of the front line at Ploegsteert Wood in Belgium, he was reported killed by the blast of a shell on October 8 the same year. Captain

Boles was posthumously awarded the Military Cross 'in recognition of distinguished and meritorious service in time of war' (*Norfolk Bugle*, Nov. 5, 1915). The bodies of him and two of his men were never found.

*

> He saith among the trumpets, Ha ha; and he smelleth the battle afar off, the thunder of the captains, and the shouting.
>
> *Job*, 39:25

In the winter of 1915, the famous music hall singer and comedienne Dorothy 'Dotty' O'Shea, 'the Wexford Warbler', was forced to abandon her lodgings in Pimlico and survive penniless for a week on the streets of London following what Ernst Cleaver in the December issue of *The Thespian* calls 'a lamentable production of *HMS Pinafore*', which was forced to close after the first performance.

In a book of conversations with the Irish journalist Patrick Malloy, imaginatively entitled *Dots and Dashes* (1951), Miss O'Shea painfully recalls the unpleasant episode, 'made all the more unbearably', she says, 'by freezing temperatures in the capital that year and excruciating toothache'.

Miss O'Shea spent much of her time in the Covent Garden area, but was forced to endure three nights sleeping rough in Trafalgar Square, where she met a young man by the name of Ed Bower who, she says, 'had been several weeks on the road and was in a considerably worse condition'.

P. Malloy: And what did yea make o' the fella?

Miss O'Shea: He looked for all the world like a scarecrow, very tall and slim with piercing blue eyes and dressed in no more than rags that might have been a uniform. I thought he was probably a disgraced priest or something as he was very knowledgeable of the Catholic faith but quite reserved. Usually we just sat in silence throughout the night, in the comfort of each other's company, but on the last evening I told him my entire history, and when I mentioned my abscess he took some sort of plant from his pocket and pressed it into the corner of my mouth, which eased the pain immediately. I was quite astonished and lost for words, but he just smiled, picked up his belongings and walked off towards the Embankment with the sun rising before him.

In November 1928, the recently appointed Rev. Stanley Jules of All Saints' Church, Mude, was preparing a sermon to commemorate the tenth anniversary of the 1918 Armistice. On the morning of the ninth, he received a letter addressed to his predecessor, the Rev. Samuel Theaks, 'accompanied by a small bundle of notebooks, tied with string and stuffed with scraps, from Mr Aubrey Stiles, who was formerly a sergeant with the Oxfordshire and Buckinghamshire Light Infantry' (*Mude Evening Courier*, Nov. 9, 1928). Stiles, who was in the process of moving to Eastbourne with his sister, had discovered the package in his attic, where it had remained hidden among a collection of his own military memorabilia for over a decade.

Sergeant A. Stiles was wounded by a sniper's bullet on July 30, shortly before an ill-fated assault well after first light at Guillemont on the Somme in 1916. The bundle was given to him by Private Edward Bowler as he was stretched from the line. Stiles describes 'an odd bloke who had a strange but most settling effect upon the company and bore a strength of character inappropriate to his rank' (Aubrey Stiles, *Letter to Rev. Samuel Theakes*, Nov. 7, 1928).

The notebooks and miscellaneous pages are hand written and contain numerous passages from the *Bible*. They are in no discernible order with some appearing several times throughout the work. Apart from the name and address of the intended recipient on one of the front covers, there is no suggestion of when or by whom they were written. A curious last entry, however, offers some indication. The page must have caught the eye of the Rev. Jules as later that day it was reproduced (with one amendment, line 13) in the town's evening paper. The form and style bear a striking resemblance to the earlier *Country Capers*, particularly 'Song o' the Season' (1908), yet the characteristic fourth verse is sadly absent.

Captain Blunder

When the whistle blew and the wheels refused,
And we all were rocked from under,
There were shrieks from the girls and thrills in the boys
As a brass band played on stronger.
We made fond farewells to a peel of bells

And the Lord whose path we wonder;
With our spirits raised we hailed and gave
Three cheers for Captain Blunder:
'Hip, hip, for Captain Blunder.'

Now we march along to a stirring song
And the distant roar of thunder,
For the battle's won with the filthy Hun
And the bastards blown asunder.
We may shade awhile in our foreign trial
But still choose to follow our Saviour,
For there stands the One in the mid-day sun
Beside our Captain Blunder.
We love you, Captain Blunder.

In a burrowed isle with the rank and file,
For it's here we quietly hunker,
We await the dawn and the coming storm,
While the mood turns still and sombre.
In our thoughts alone, of loved ones back home
And a foe we're sure to conquer,
We kneel and pray till the break of day:
'Where art thou, Captain Blunder?
'God save you, Captain Blunder.'

Information on Edward Bowler is scarce. He enlisted on April 12, 1916, and was immediately sent to the front. A brief account of the attack on Guillemont, in which his name appears, is given by General Sir George H. Mullan, who was then a corporal with the same battalion:

Supporting action had left the forward German posts untouched for we advanced against scything machine-gun fire in which it seemed nothing could live. Upon reaching the relative calm of the station, I found Private E. Bowler kneeling beside Second-Lieutenant R.W. Holmes, a man of outstanding promise who was already dead. Private Bowler's right arm had been shot away and there were other wounds to his right side. As he turned to me his lower jaw swung loose by the left hinge. *A Life*, vol. ii (1950)

Bowler died shortly after mid-day on July 30, 1916. His body lies in the British sector of war dead at the local cemetery. There is no record of any allied officer with the name 'Captain Blunder' serving in World War One.

*

To every thing there is a season, and a time to every purpose under the heaven. *Ecclesiastes*, 3:1

On September 7, 1940, the weekly *Capital Dispatch*, below the astonishing headline 'SURPRISING SAINTLY SPECTACLE', reported that 'curious lights' had been seen early on two consecutive Sunday mornings above the church of St Martin-in-the-Fields in London. The first occasion, it is said, was witnessed only by the church verger Hollis Binns, who had been enjoying 'a friendly rubber of bridge when he was forced to return to the church for his wallet and found the building momentarily bathed in light'.

The second incident, the paper records, was observed by 'a crowd of more than a dozen', among whom was the respected diarist and thinker Horace T. Glean, who refers to the event as 'a sporadic supernatural sight' (*Jottings*, Jun.-Sep. 1940), although he fails to comment further or offer any explanation for the event.

Coincidently, on the day that the article appeared a short funeral service was held in the church for an elderly gentleman known locally as 'Dewdrop', so called because he always carried a drop of moisture from the end of his nose that apparently froze into a tiny icicle in cold weather. The man had been found dead in the waiting room of Victoria Station on the day before and was identified from his possessions as Isaiah Boles, husband to the late Sarah and father of the missing Edwin.

After separating from his family, Isaiah Boles seems also to have parted company with England and may have lived among the Society of Friends in Philadelphia, Pennsylvania. The date of his departure for the United States is uncertain, but he returned to England in August 1930, and lived homeless on the streets of London for the remainder of his life.

The service was a poorly attended affair and was prolonged primarily for the benefit of Miss S. Forbes, the discoverer of the body, Mr William 'Corker' Mackenzie, stationmaster at Victoria, and the soon-to-be Rev. Colin P. Loveless of St Augustine's, Colchester, who was apparently 'in dire need of the practice' (*StMF, Church Committee Minutes*, 'Any

Other Business', September 6, 1940).

Shortly before the service began, the Rev. Loveless met 'a strange man, perhaps on leave, sitting deep in prayer at the rear of the church, and who, when asked, seemed to know a great deal about the deceased' (*London's Churchmen*, vol. iv, ed. Timothy T. Tanner, 1962). In his interview with the above publication, Hollis Binns continues:

> The reverend spoke with the man for several minutes until they were joined by a young woman with a northern accent. She was dressed in working clothes, which the reverend considered quite unsuitable for the occasion. The two were obviously more interested in each other than with the proceedings, and the reverend, recognising he was unwanted in their company, or that he was perhaps the victim of some practical joke, discreetly retreated to the vestry.
>
> Amazingly and to everyone's annoyance, the couple remained in conversation throughout the service and similarly disgrace themselves with the emanation of embarrassing sniggers, fits of giggles and even shrieks of laughter during the eulogy. The Rev. Loveless was forced on more than one occasion to remind the perpetrators whose house it was they were in and, if they had no desire to behave in a respectable manner, he was quite certain that the entire congregation would be eternally grateful if they would please leave immediately.

> The pair sat firm, persisting with their outbursts, and when the service was concluded the Rev. Loveless would surely have delivered to them a stinging rebuke had they not already fled the building.

Binns' account is certainly disturbing, but it is largely overshadowed by later events in the day – as the first bombs of the Blitz began to fall on London. In the horror that followed heroes would arise by accident and from the most unlikely quarters, and although all accounts are fascinating one in particular deserves notice.

At the time George Parsons was a 56-year-old insurance clerk, a local Rotarian and part-time A.R.P. warden on the Strand. In writing to his immediate superior, Parsons reports 'a disgraceful infringement of the blackout', which he 'confronted alone and at great personal risk', regardless of the fact that he had 'expressly arranged to be off duty on the night in question' (George Parsons, *Letter to Brig-Gen T.C. Sims (rtd)*, Sep. 8, 1940). Parsons continues:

> At approximately five o'clock in the evening, while returning from a most enjoyable afternoon with my dear cousin Winifred, I found myself in the company of Mr Gordon Fennel, assistant manager of a specialised and highly respected musical instrument store, Mrs Jacky Peabody and her daughter Caroline from Brighton, who had spent the day 'doing the sights', as they put it, Mr Albert Cotter, a local tradesman and

occasional (although not as often as he would like) course sportsman, Mr Wilfred Stevens, a retired painter and decorator, and his good lady wife Beryl, all of whom I had the pleasure to meet while sheltering in the basement of Pierce & Co., 'Grand Pianos', est. 1921, at the lower end of the Charring Cross Road.

Mr Fennel was in the process of locking the building when the raid began, and those of us unfortunate to find ourselves at the mercy of the Luftwaffe, but lucky enough to be in the vicinity of the above premises, raced for the doors, much to the surprise of Mr Fennel.

There we remained for the evening and, although morale waned on several occasions, the majority sustained themselves with Mr Cotter's timely discovery of six bottles of a seemingly excellent Madeira and Mrs Peabody's rousing medley of popular show tunes, which she performed on an apparently irreplaceable Steinway, again to the dismay of Mr Fennel.

At about three o'clock in the morning I felt the bombing ease a little and, as the only one of our group still conscious, I ascended the ladder to the main shop in what I now recognise was a reckless act of brazen inquisitiveness. There was, however, nothing to see through the shop's front window except thick waves of acrid smoke that swept in from the East End, and I could only imagine the subsequent devastation from the sound of many distant explosions, alarms, collapsing masonry and more bombs screaming towards earth.

I moved away from the window in great despondence and was about to descend the ladder when I noticed that the smoke was beginning to clear. The sky was bright red and filled with flying sparks and burning embers. I went again to the window perfectly mesmerised by the sight. Suddenly a thin radiant beam of blue light appeared and shone upwards from St Martin's. Shortly after it was joined by a second and then a third, all twisting together.

Not knowing what they were, but judging they must surely be an obvious assistance to the raiders, I unlocked the shop door and, with no thought for my safety, sprinted across the road, up the front steps and began pounding on the church doors, while conveying my anxiety for the situation in no uncertain terms. I received no response and stood back from the building again looking up.

Within the beams there appeared three other lights of such brightness that I was forced to shield my eyes. The three spun and rose in unison, and when they were out of view the beams were extinguished.

This, I thought, was an end to the matter, but as I walked away the church doors were thrown open and I saw the building illuminated inside. To my astonishment a congregation of about a hundred people walked calmly out into the street to the accompaniment of soft music and with no apparent care for the present emergency. My efforts to obtain any explanation for the event were blindly ignored, and as the smoke returned I was forced back into the shop.

In the morning I cautioned the church verger, a secretive and, in my opinion, thoroughly disreputable character, who told me that the building had been securely locked at 3.45 that afternoon and had not been opened since. Nor, he said, was any service held during the night.

This, I know, is untrue and although it is not my intention to interfere with a private ceremony, nor prove disrespectful towards any manner of worship, surely there is a time and a place for everything.

What exactly George Parsons and others saw that summer remains a mystery. However, as early as spring 1940, it was rumoured among German pilots that the British War Office had developed a sophisticated anti-aircraft weapon that could disrupt the electronics of enemy planes. Initially the device, code named ‘Messiah’, was a visual warning intended to dissuade pilots from flying over key targets. In action, however, and if successful the weapon might cripple an aircraft and cause it to fall on a highly populated area. The papers relating to ‘Messiah’ are held by the Public Record Office and remain classified. They are not due to be released until New Year’s Day, 2041.

Correspondence

Dear Sir/Madam

I am writing to...

a. *complain about a recent article in your publication.*

b. *offer my congratulations for what I regard as a first-class example of professional journalism.*

(*Title*) by (*name*) of (*date*) is, to my knowledge, the most provocative enquiry ever to appear in print. To say that I was surprised to find this issue addressed with such candour and originality would grossly underestimate my reaction.

(*Title*) exhibits an astonishing level of research, while the content and presentation are nothing short of remarkable.

Mr/Ms (*name*) evidently demonstrates a unique and extraordinary talent and is obviously familiar with a side of his/her subject that I, until now, was blissfully unaware. His/her inimitable prose style a. *simply trips* b. *trips simply* off the page and vividly reflects his/her aptitude for the written word. Mr/Ms (*name*)'s attention to detail is no less astounding (and to a degree that I would scarcely have thought possible), while his/her ability to arouse strong emotions within the reader is beyond my comprehension. Opposing views and contradictory arguments apparently present no obstacle to this journalist as seemingly irrefutable evidence, from many varied and respected sources, is effortlessly and relentlessly dismissed in a single line. To put it mildly, the level of affinity between Mr/Ms (*name*) and his/her chosen profession is quite simply staggering!

I have often been affected by an article in your publication but never responded in this way before. On this occasion, however, moved almost to tears and still reeling from the experience, I am compelled to vent my opinion.

May I say that the standard of writing you continually purvey never ceases to amaze me. Words alone simply fail to express my feelings for the calibre of work you and your staff ceaselessly produce.

Yours sincerely...

Doctor Wagner
(abridged version)

Letter XXVI
To Miss Matheson, England

5 May, 9.42pm

My dearest Emily,-

It has been an entire day since my last communication, and almost a whole week from leaving my beloved's side and England's shores, yet in all that time nothing can compare to the dreadful events of the interim, the very thought of which now induces me to shudder and my hands to tremble with such ferocity that I am scarcely able to pen a single line.

You may recall my initial encounter with Helga, Herr whatever his-name-is, the hotel manager's eldest stepdaughter, whose spacious and (I would venture to say) sumptuous apartment, I was surprised to discover, shares an adjoining door to my modest yet homely accommodation. Other than my immediate and sincere apology, upon which, if you will permit me to reiterate, I did later elaborate in a comprehensive account before the hotel manager and assembled members of his family and staff (a written transcript of which I have since lodged with the hotel's receptionist), I have had nothing further to do with the girl in question. That is, and pray do not alarm yourself, my dear, for on this occasion I am completely innocent of impropriety, until this morning.

I was aroused early from the deepest slumber by a thunderous commotion in the adjacent room. Having recently grown accustomed to the morning manners that prevail in many, if not all, continental hotels I was not unduly alarmed, however, the magnitude of this latest disturbance was quite unprecedented in my experience and so prolonged that it became impossible for any conscientious soul to innocently ignore. Therefore, reluctantly I was compelled to rise and, when decently attired, make haste with my investigations as to its origin.

It was with a certain degree of caution and some trepidation that I tentatively approached on my toes the door beyond which evidently lay the source of the uproar. There I hesitated and suddenly thought it more discreet (if not advisable considering my most recent indiscretion) to advance upon the scene indirectly, from the corridor, in fear that I may again invite erroneous accusations of expedient intrusion or, indeed, implicate myself in I knew not what by the circumstantial proximity of my quarters to the ensuing fracas. Thus, the chair, positioned the night before to prevent trespass and preserve my privacy, remained securely fast under the curiously ornate but stalwart handle of this troublesome partition.

With my heart pounding at a rate that I felt certain would expire at any moment, and perspiring profusely in anxious anticipation of what fate lay in store, I ventured forth from my chamber and out onto the landing.

As I advanced down the passage I came upon the rear of a large and agitated assembly that, confined on either side by decorative walls, appeared to represent the entire complement of hotel personnel. By the way, it may interest you to know that this incongruent troop includes all manner of obscure tradesmen and providers of service who are essential to facilitate the efficient and successful administration of such an establishment. In addition, as if the multitude before me was insufficient to contain the household's most frightful nocturnal catastrophe, I also found the majority of hotel guests, many of whom were no less hysterical but, in my opinion, immodestly dressed for the occasion.

On closer inspection I discovered that the crowd gathered before me was not arranged at random, nor stationed without any apparent purpose, as I had first surmised, but instead was most orderly (at least in its entirety if not in its constituent parts). Indeed, all present were currently engaged in a peculiar system of rotation, whereby the foremost member would enter the room beside mine only to emerge a few moments later, after the emission of a seemingly obligatory exclamation, to be consoled by the preceding combatant dissolved in tears or carrying a grotesque countenance of mortified petrifaction induced, I could only imagine, by the hideous spectacle formerly witnessed within.

So preoccupied was the multitude with this tumultuous discovery, my approach towards its centre went completely unnoticed and without hindrance.

Confident by now that my arrival within the throng was of no consequence to the matter in hand, I pressed deeper into the group enthused, I would suggest, by a compassionate desire to lend assistance, if required, but equally (and it shames me to say this) by my own insatiable curiosity. However, quite suddenly and to my dismay, as I rose from within and strained on my points at the very seat of the action (in a vain attempt to observe that which lay obscured before me), my presence was acknowledged and instantly sounded by a monstrous ejaculation from the hotel manager's wife, Frau Hilda or Hildegard, I believe, a formidable woman of substance, whose shoulder I had discreetly employed with the tip of my index finger for no other purpose than to steady my footing in what had degenerated into a boisterous environment of acute claustrophobia. I recoiled from my verbal assailant with equal consternation and, like a brute from the traps, took to my heels and fled headlong down the corridor, hotly pursued, I might add, by a murderous rabble, armed to the teeth with a terrifying arsenal of buckets, mops, a variety of kitchen utensils (the purpose of which still alludes me) and even, if memory serves, a garden spade, each to a man hell-bent on my destruction. Indeed, were it not for the timely intervention of the hotel manager (with whom, in flight, I did unwittingly collide), who then hurried me into my room while conveying his assurance that there was no cause for alarm, I would surely have been lost to the mob. Once more I was forced to remonstrate my innocence and again implore that no deception was intended, but my overtures were rejected, albeit politely, for the door closed calmly before me and I was left sitting on the corner of my bed in utter bewilderment of the frantic and, to my ear, unintelligible deliberations that had since broken out in the corridor beyond the door.

Considering the explicit hostility with which I had been greeted, I could only assume that the heated exchanges now in progress must certainly relate to me, but as to the calamitous occurrence that had befallen this dwelling to incite such a homicidal temper among its inhabitants, raised to a fever unimaginable in England, I could only surmise; nor was I privy to a debate that centred on some as yet unknown tragic act that lay but a few feet from my person and in which I, to all and sundry, was the principal suspect.

Not for the first time in my travels, nor should I think the last, did I reside in absolute confusion, unable to reason the behaviour of foreigners, and although, as you are aware, I am not easily affronted, I believe there is no shame in admitting to you, my dearest, that this Englishman, who would otherwise have dismissed the event as an unpleasant demonstration of emotional laxity, where it not for the fact that he again had become the inadvertent victim of circumstance, was shocked to the very marrow of his being. Indeed, such was his surprise, the gentleman at issue was thrown into a state of acute delirium that induced an absurd posture of semi-paralysis for a period of somewhere between twenty minutes and half an hour.

At length I recovered, although my composure was not yet restored (and still, I might add, remains but a shadow of its former self). Meanwhile, with no obvious sign of imminent insurgence, with the neighbouring cogitations abating and I still fragile from the rudest interruption to my sleep, I decided to avail myself of the mild soporific that your dear mother was kind enough to press upon me at my departure and weather out the storm.

When next I awoke, again with your dear likeness at my bedside to serve as the only reassurance of normality, my initial thought was that the entire occurrence had been nothing more than a hideous dream from which I was now blissfully emancipated. Although, of course, I knew it to be a fallacy, I played for some time in this comforting delusion and behaved throughout my morning toilet as if nothing untoward had occurred.

It was only when admiring the small and delightfully constructed timepiece on the wall above my dressing table, an exquisite creation of Albrecht Hertzog & Co., a local and highly respected firm of clock and watch manufactures, whose premises are situated approximately forty minutes by carriage from the centre of town, and who offer guided tours of the factory from April to September daily (except Sunday) at no charge, although in the summer months it is advisable to arrange an appointment, I suddenly gasped for breath, as:

'Good heavens!' I exclaimed aloud, it was now 10.30 and half the morning gone already. The carriage that would have conveyed me to the home of my client had certainly left promptly at 9.00, as I was assured it would by the hotel's receptionist, a man of great exactness with the finest (yet, to my eye, sadly illegible) copperplate that I have so far encountered abroad. Consequently and with no alternative course of action available, I was resigned to endure the entire day in idleness and forced to spend yet another night of possible disruption in this otherwise charming abode. Furthermore, the despair of my predicament was made all the worse when I realised that my good name and character, as testified at length in numerous letters of recommendation, composed in all sincerity by some of the most respected members of my profession, would be justly sullied in the estimation of my client with whom I should have to engage this very evening; a commitment sealed in all good faith through extensive correspondence, but now, due to my own lethargy and the region's inexpensive and reliable, but lamentably infrequent, transportation system, that promise was impossible to fulfil. Therefore, like a hunted prey, I remained silent in my room in mortal fear of the consequences should I again alight – and the morning elapsed before me.

By mid-day I became susceptible to the pangs of hunger, as I had missed breakfast, which is served between 6.00 and 8.30 in the morning and is not included in the cost of the room. While I wondered of what this meal might consist and deliberated over the possibility of a refund, having paid in advance for the privilege and specifically reserved a table in the somewhat uninspiring yet serviceable dining-room but failed to make an appearance, there was a knock at the door.

It came again, the first having startled me so much that I was for a moment unable to utter a single word. Eventually, however, I found my tongue and managed to permit entrance on the third and, by this time, insistent occasion.

There appeared at the door the hotel manager and some sort of police constable or military officer, an officious little character who was presently cultivating an elaborate moustache on his upper lip, although the eventual form of this commendable and, to my mind, highly ambitious undertaking remained uncertain. By way of a consolation, however, he did demonstrate a basic grasp of the English language, which is more than can be said of anyone else in this country. As I have told you before, the people of this region will persistently occupy their time in idle chatter, which is then reduced to covert whispers as you approach, and, if asked directions, they are either stuck dumb on the spot or offensively grunt at you to the accompaniment of flamboyant gestures that, to the uninitiated and with unfaltering success, convey precisely nothing. I can only hope, as I am reasonably assured, that my client is a man of some quality and a breed apart from what I have so far discovered among the common rabble who seem intent on rubbishing the visitor with their loathsome hostility and brutal acts of public humiliation.

Following the briefest introduction (either that or

the hotel manager was clearing an obstruction in his throat), the constable embarked on a series of rudimentary questions and, given the obvious severity of his inquiry, I obliged him in answering honestly and to the best of my knowledge (although, duty bound, I discreetly withheld any inference of my client's identity). When we had dispensed with the preliminaries, a necessary but demeaning procedure that would have more than adequately established my immediate exoneration from this squalid affair by any competent inquisitor at home without, I might add, having to subject my credentials to thorough scrutiny or the hotel manager's benevolent but auxiliary interjections, I was then informed of what had earlier occurred, and again fear not, for I will certainly omit any explicit and distressing details so as not to alarm my darling.

As I understand the matter, Fraulein something-or-other, a humble chambermaid in the consummation of her morning labours, following an unresponsive forewarning at the door and with the assistance of a passkey, entered Helga's room at around 7.15 and, to her dismay, discovered the poor child sprawled lifeless on the bed in what can only be described as (and do prepare yourself for the phrase, my dear) a nefarious state of undress.

Now, I have recently heard that it is not unusual for hotel staff to stumble upon a scene of private indignity or personal intimacy. Indeed, at such time in the morning the probability of subservient incursion is so fortuitous that, while effecting his duties, discretion should always be foremost in the mind of the diligent staff member. What is more, if engaged by any self-respecting establishment, he will have been cautioned of the phenomenon and, in the event, subsequently advised to profit nothing by way of futile excuses or elaborate protestations, but instead to immediately retreat from the scene and only return after the duration of a respectable interlude. However, on this occasion, the girl in question, being of feeble disposition (a characteristic that I have always believed is irreconcilable with a curious mind) and prone to open displays of abandon, was so effected by what she saw immediately issued an uproarious racket that awoke the household to her cause and, presumably, as she fled from the building in terror, the entire neighbourhood. I am told that even now this wretched creature has yet to regain her senses.

It was shortly after this that I, with the greatest regret, entered the thick of the fray and inflamed an already volatile atmosphere of malicious conjecture. Eventually, however, and in my absence, a semblance of sanity was restored and officers of the law were summoned to attend post-haste, upon whose arrival the most senior (with whom I was presently in conference) confirmed everyone's worse suspicions that devilish work was afoot.

I confessed to hearing nothing during the night having (it pities me to say) somewhat overindulged the previous evening in the hospitality of the hotel manager who, for no apparent reason, has taken a liking to my person and chooses to look favourably upon me.

The constable, or whatever he was (his exact rank escapes me), strutted about the room postulating and gesticulating to suggest that it was more than his moustache that was causing him irritation. Finally, and mercifully for the carpet on which he relentlessly trod, he shrugged his shoulders, made some terse comment under his breath and left the room, although not before stepping over his colleagues who now lay at his feet having spilled in from the corridor when he had opened the door.

While I was sitting in silence with the hotel manager, desperately wishing to convey some sentiment of condolence but knowing that any attempt of sympathetic articulation on my part would invariably fall on deaf ears, the strangest thing occurred. Interestingly, this startling assertion confirms my theory that all foreigners are perfectly capable of speaking English when it suits them, and that they only pretend not to understand the language for their own sense of perverted gratification – the blackguard spoke to me! He did indeed, confound the man, in all eloquence with just a trace of his native accent.

'I beg your pardon,' I stammered, fearing that his oration had been the work of some invisible phantom hovering about us for sport, or perhaps just a fancy of mine. 'Did you say something?'

'Strange times, Herr English,' he repeated, on this occasion supplementing his statement with the loathsome address that has acquired widespread popularity since my arrival, and although I deplore being referred to by this ludicrous appellation, I have regrettably conceded in allowing it to pass unchallenged if only for the sake of diplomacy.

'Indeed!' I exclaimed. 'Very strange,' referring more to the elaborate charade to which I had not been privy than to the alarming events of the morning.

Again there was silence, but after a moment, as I considered what had driven him to this explosion of linguistic propensity, I thought I heard him mutter: 'They have none of the *close*,' which I felt required additional explanation and decided, least the meaning of his utterance haunt me for the rest of my days, to attain further clarification if only to appease my soul.

'The what, sorry?' I asked.

'*Clothes*,' it sounded like, and was certainly probable given the exposed condition of the girl's discovery, but with a little deduction on my part and considering the circumstances of our conversation, I hazarded a guess as to the gist of his unease.

'Oh, *clues*, you mean. Is that what you're trying to say? They have no *clues*, the police, as to the cause of death.'

'Ya, ya,' he repeated (which means 'yes, yes' to us and is actually spelt: ja, ja), 'you are right – no clues.'

'I see. Well, this is a pickle, isn't it?'

'Pickle?' he enquired.

'Pickle, yes. No? Oh dear. Well, it's a sort of stew one gets into, you know? A real pea-souper, what?' I then emitted a short burst of laughter to lighten the burden of his confusion but eventually dropped the subject believing it incommodious to elucidate further on my euphemisms. Instead, I cunningly steered his thinking towards speculation of what possible motive might lie behind poor Helga's untimely demise, rudely dispatched from this world, as indeed she was, and from under our very noses. However, try as we might, neither the hotel manager nor even I could shed any light upon the mystery, and furthermore he informed me that the local police, when deliberating upon these sordid episodes of uncertain misadventure, as I had first surmised, were nothing short of useless.

In total bewilderment I turned to the window for inspiration and found in the view offered a scene of harmonious tranquillity that would surly contrast with the one now bolted fast in the room next door. All was calm and bright and very peaceful in the streets below, where a depleted populace had succumbed to news of the tragedy, which had spread like a feverish rash throughout the town and brought a renewed urgency to their doings. Gone were the customary pavement loiterings, the casual perambulations and leisurely exchanges of social intercourse between the locals. Many of the nearby shops were closed. Few ventured abroad and those who did moved swiftly and timid, often stopping furtively in doorways (to ensure that the next stage of their progress would pass unhindered) before hurriedly continuing upon their journey. Above the red corrugated tile roofs, a common feature of the region that has largely replaced the antiquated thatch, although one can still find examples of the tradition on the outskirts of town and, during August and September when the work of restoration is in progress, they are, I am told, well worth a visit, ominous clouds loomed far in the distance, while high on the cliff face a light mist circled below a dark and imposing structure, apparently the home of some renowned local dignitary whose title escapes me for the moment.

Returning to my immediate surroundings and no further forward in resolving our troubles, I tried to remember the name of a little known detective in London, a pugnacious fellow with a chequered history but the instincts of a terrier, who has been engaged by our office on more than one occasion with much success to his credit.

While I considered the practicalities of transporting 'Mr Grimes', for I am almost certain that that is his name, to the scene, but fearing the consequences should the unconventional behaviour of this obstinate and doggedly sleuth prove too advanced for the inquiry, and I having vouched for his character with only a modicum of satisfaction, the hotel manager offered an altogether more convenient alternative. In what I now believe was sheer desperation, he informed me of a scholarly but reclusive gentleman who lived locally, was widely experienced in such matters and may, in return for a nominal imbursement, grace us with his presence. I then discovered that the hotel manager had already made the same suggestion to the police constable who, typically and obviously affronted by the proposal, had dismissed the idea unreservedly and steadfastly refused to engage with what he must have thought would prove a rival investigation. The hotel manager then left the room in apparent distress, and I took it upon myself to seek out the gentleman in whom he had placed so much confidence – if only as some small restitution for his kindness.

After a ponderous luncheon of over-cured meat, an unrecognisable form of greens and a few measly under boiled potatoes, a derisorily offering of persistent turgidity in a portion that fell woefully short of the cost, I strode out of the hotel and into the afternoon sunlight in search of the elusive consultant.

Now, to those in the know, which is practically everyone in town, the name Doctor Wagner possesses the unique capability of instigating uncontrollable hysterics, fevered convulsions or blind panic at a single utterance. I surmised from what the hotel manager had told me that this notorious practitioner was indeed a remarkable fellow whose infamy lay, I wagered to myself, in the ability to be all things to all men. To one he was a genius, to another a prophet, to a third a shaman, to a fourth a dangerous lunatic and so on, and gradually I came to realise that 'Doctor Wagner' was actually more of an idea than a man: a fanatical religion or complex ideology whose principles were constantly shifting to err on the side of convenience. It is just possibly that 200 years from now there will be a statue of Doctor Wagner adorning the town square and venerating his methods, whereas 200 years ago he would certainly have been burnt at the stake. I, however, held no undue optimism in his ability, but nor was I about to condemn the man's integrity until I had met him for myself and judged his nature accordingly.

I had enquired of his whereabouts from the hotel's receptionist who, following a moment's hesitation whilst I patiently cajoled a response, quite unexpectedly spluttered part of the meal that he was in the process of consuming in my direction. After drying my face with a freshly laundered handkerchief, a service that is provided daily and at no extra charge, I was for some time at pains to remove a crumb of this repast from the corner of my eye. I withdrew from the desk in silence and disgust, while the receptionist tumbled in my estimation. I was, however, surprisingly more fortunate with some loafer who was sitting fast asleep, dressed in ridiculous apparel (which supposedly passes for the national costume), with his bare legs stretched impassably across the vestibule. Although initially a dismal prospect, once awake it took no effort at all to have him inform me that my objective lay down a narrow wynd to the right of the main road that runs the length of the town. I should point out here that any knowledge street names is of no value whatsoever and serves only to hinder the visitor's progress. There are few signs to indicate the names of streets, and those that do exist, I am convinced, are regularly changed for others by the locals for amusement.

I had been walking for only a few minutes, as instructed by the doorman, if that is in fact his position, when I found myself completely lost and unable to find my way back to the hotel, where, if the doorman had not relapsed into the arms of Morpheus, I might obtain further clarification of his directions.

It is worth remembering that many members of staff, particularly in some of the larger hotels on the Continent, have the tendency to display an avid willingness to assist unconditionally upon one's arrival, yet this enthusiasm tends to wane with familiarity and can often border on contempt. I believe in all sincerity that the extension of any modest sojourn beyond a week would sadly result in the inability to obtain even the time of day from the lowliest domestic.

Undaunted and resolved to conclude my venture, I determined to collar the next passing townsman and demand, by what ever means necessary, that he reveal to me the whereabouts of not only myself but also the home of the esteemed man of science in whom the hotel manager had entrusted all faith imaginable.

Just as I was about to pounce on an unsuspecting peasant who was labouring towards me under a yoke with two large wooden buckets suspended by rope from either end, I suddenly heard a voice that I recognised shouting my name – or at least its corrupted form.

Interestingly, the yoke with twin buckets descending, known locally as 'das Tragjoch', from which the hotel derives its name, is the town's emblem and is exquisitely replicated in a motif of finely carved sandstone above the main door of the town hall. Many lesser examples of the same (including that embossed here on the hotel's good quality stationery) can be found above the entrances to some shops and private dwellings; the townsfolk having conspicuously embraced the symbol and the incredulous fable from which it originates.

The story, as was recounted to me last evening by a fanatical travelling salesman of mixed parentage, whose name was something wholly unpronounceable, centres on a lonely dairymaid living on a dilapidated farm with her work-shy father, who must trek each day through perilous woods on her way to town where she might peddle her wares in return for a meagre income. The simple song that she sings while about her frugal enterprise is similarly woeful and, from what I could gather from the travelling salesman, roughly translates as:

> Oh what a terrible thing it is to be carrying these heavy buckets of milk through dangerous woods all the way to town for what amounts to not very much at all, and me with a lazy father to look after back home. Will someone buy my milk?

(I will play to you the delightful tune of accompaniment when I return, as I made a point of committing it to memory.)

One day, while returning home more sorrowful than usual, the poor maid strays from the path and stumbles upon a savage wolf whose leg is caught in a trap. The maid takes pity on the beast, offers it some of the milk that was left over from the day's trading, as business that day had been particularly bad, and releases the creature from its restraints. Having licked its wounds, the wolf then turns into a handsome buck of a lad who takes an immediate liking to the girl. The yoke and buckets are thrown to the four winds and the pair are never heard of again. The idle father, who must now support himself, discovers talents that were erstwhile dormant within him. He promptly sets himself up in business manufacturing his own design of rocking chair, which has a patented action and is operated by a series of declining weights that requires the least effort to manipulate. The chairs are still sold today having changed little from their original conception and, I am told, are extremely reasonable in price, although these days one must allow at least one month's duration before delivery. (I have it on good authority that 'a superb middle-of-the-range model', apparently 'the choice of the discerning consumer', as it is described in the firm's literature, should arrive at the home of great-aunt Hester shortly before her 75th birthday on the 23rd of next month.)

The father becomes a wealthy man and is made the equivalent of the town's mayor, Burger-something-or-other, but he is soon ousted from office following the discovery of human remains on his former property.

The voice behind me, if you will remember, was that of none other than the somnolent doorman, who had followed me possibly fearing the incursion of my displeasure should I return to the hotel unsuccessful in my expedition. Regardless of his erroneous address, I was grateful for any opportune salutation as, simultaneously, I was forced to remove myself from the main thoroughfare while the approaching menial shuffled passed me without the slightest acknowledgment of my presence. I firmly believe that were it not for doorman's timely intervention I would certainly be standing there yet.

As it happened I was but a street away from my quarry, and although the doorman was good enough to escort me to the corner, he would not accompany me further and turned quite pale at the suggestion before hurrying away out of sight. Like Theseus at the gates of the Labyrinth about to confront the dreadful Minotaur, I stood at the entrance to a dark and narrow passage where I straightened my spine, braced the collar of my topcoat against the back of my neck and stepped valiantly into the unknown.

Ever cautious where I made my footing I was instantly struck by a sweet pungent fragrance that pervaded the air. The buildings on either side appeared to close in above my head, as each progressive storey was evidently more spacious than its predecessor, while the sky beyond became nothing but a thin strip of blue that offered no assistance when walking on what purported to be the pavement.

About half way down I was hailed by three charming ladies who were leaning out the windows of a large but dilapidated building. They appeared to be a very cheerful group and, as I understood their convivial gestures, were inviting me inside for what I gathered was a little light refreshment. Politely, and perhaps regrettably for they were some of the few people in this town who have so far shown any interest in my person (and although one may be willing to make the acquaintance of foreigners, one's approaches are not always reciprocated), I declined much to their disappointment.

Further on, however, after some slight confusion with an extremely well-dressed gentleman who was obviously in a great hurry to be somewhere else, I found the Doctor's house without any difficulty and identified the said residence by an engraved brass plaque beside the door. 'DOKTOR WAGNER', it said – but nothing more.

I hesitated for a moment and looked about me not wishing to be observed. Suddenly a cry rang out from an upper floor and as I looked up a pail of foul smelling water was emptied directly above me. I managed to avoid the deluge to the evident amusement of a toothless hag who was sheltering on the opposite side of the lane. Yet she soon fell silent and turned quite sullen when I got to my feet and resolutely pulled at the doorbell, which sent her scurrying off into the distance like a wounded harpy.

The household was obviously not expecting any visitors, for at length a gormless manservant of about thirty-five appeared behind the coloured glass in the door (a typical feature of town houses, although this was not a particularly fine example). Eventually, however, and following a little encouragement, he revealed himself while buttoning up his collar stud and pushing an arm into his jacket. He did not understand a word I said, nor I him, so I offered my card, which he snatched from my grasp, pretended to read and then, with some reluctance, showed me into the library just as a young scullery maid, who was replacing an apron about her waist, leapt from the room in some distress and disappeared below stairs. I glanced knowingly at the butler, who gave no indication that anything untoward had occurred. I, too, chose to ignore the incident fearing that any demand for an explanation would only complicate or further delay my mission.

The butler left me alone to examine the room and its contents. The high ceiling demonstrated some ornate cornice work and was set above three walls of books, while the fourth held six leaded windows that looked out over a neglected courtyard. The only furniture in the room was a beaten leather armchair, a set of library steps and an enormous oval table that was heaped to capacity with numerous wooden packing cases, some of which had been opened to expose the rough straw that protected the items within. I carefully pushed my hand through the stuffing in one of the smaller boxes and pulled out a glass vessel containing a cloudy liquid and some form of specimen that I was unable to identify. After critical examination of the object and growing slightly concerned, if not disturbed, by the Doctor's interests, I replaced the jar in its box and turned my attention to the shelves. I was, however, permitted only an introductory perusal, although I did have time to briefly encounter a considerable body of work pertaining to every known aspect of occultish practices and diabolical behaviour.

As I became quite mesmerised by the sight of these curious volumes the two beautifully inlaid doors to the library, which depicted some sort of histrionic Grecian theme, were suddenly thrown open and in a flourish there entered a robust character of middle years and portly stature, whose ruddy complexion was made all the more conspicuous by a full white beard and shoulder-length hair to match. He was dressed (if dressed be the word) in a pair of old carpet slippers that were flattened at the heels, astounding auburn gaiters, copious knee breeches, a white cloth shirt with emerald cravat and a red velvet smoking jacket that had obviously seen better days. In addition, this astonishing apparel was enhanced by a large curvaceous tobacco pipe and pince-nez, while the whole ensemble was topped with a corpulent beige turban and scarlet tarboosh.

'Doctor Wagner?' I ventured hesitantly.

'Herr English!' he exclaimed to my utter consternation.

He approached smiling warmly, holding my card in his pipe hand and began furiously pumping my right arm with the other, a vigorous salutation from which I was forced to extricate myself with some difficulty before he slapped me on the back and sent me hurtling across the room.

'I am most delighted to meet you. I once visited your country several years ago in the guise of unofficial ambassador, a most enjoyable vacation regrettably curtailed by affairs of state.'

'Really?' I replied, recovering from his initial assault. 'How interesting,' but I did not enquire further believing that the precise details of the matter would be confidential and improper to pursue.

'The young Prince Ogbert, an impressionable lad

from the Royal House of Ongsk, had been lead astray on a hunting trip by a mercenary gypsy and required the sternest correction.'

'Indeed!' I said and began circling the table, wishing to keep some form of physical barrier between the Doctor and myself in mortal fear of another unprovoked attack.

'I see that you are admiring my recently acquired samples. I have just returned from a hazardous but most instructive voyage around the Mediterranean where, in Arabia, I was convinced by local tribesmen that the waters of the Dead Sea contain restorative properties. Each quart of liquid requires precisely one ounce of matured fertiliser from an obliging camel to activate the minerals. I take three spoonfuls before breakfast and the same at night. The proof, Sir, is before your eyes but as yet insufficient for those learned men of our esteemed Academy.'

'Doctor Wagner, I was wondering if you would be willing to offer your opinion on a matter of some delicacy.'

'Certainly! Nothing would give me greater pleasure. No doubt you have heard of me from the indebted relations of Amadeus Gleeb, the great Swiss composer and socialite who recently suffered an unfortunate loss when the innkeeper of his local tavern carelessly relieved him of both thumbs while he sat playing at the pianoforte. All was thought lost for the boy until I, Doctor Wagner, successfully transplanted the same from a recently deceased cobbler.'

'No,' I muttered with mounting anxiety for his state

of mind and in acute awareness that my visit was fast becoming a dreadful mistake.

'Perhaps then from our very own Gustav Plotch, the respected chancellor who I rescued from Spanish itch with a hot poultice of my own devising, although regrettably his middles perished without trace, at no great loss to his wife, I might add, who has already born nine children by him and expressed no desire to embark on a tenth.'

'I'm afraid not.'

'Cardinal Muncie of Nice, perhaps, successfully recovered from acute constipation by means of persuasive purgatives and a moderate electric charge. After three days on the bench, His Eminence was rewarded with a memorable evacuation.'

'Doctor Wagner.'

'Gabby Fenwick of Prague, a hopeless inebriate restored to sanity on a strict diet of stewed cabbage and hard physical work administered at gunpoint. My methods may be unorthodox but I can assure you, Herr English, they are usually effective. My reputation, however, is the burden of my life as once more I see that I am required to officiate in yet another episode of human misfortune. Do not tell me,' he exclaimed in earnest, 'let me guess – I am also psychic.'

The Doctor, if indeed he is qualified as such, for I was beginning to have the gravest doubts, then threw himself into the most extraordinary trance that was accompanied by incomprehensible ramblings and wild convulsions.

'Ah!' he said, finally regaining consciousness. 'The

spirits vie for my attention. So much to do and so little time. Now then, what seems to be the trouble?'

Following a little background information that I felt pertinent to impart, I began my story from the moment when I first arrived in town late yesterday afternoon. The Doctor, who sat slumped in the armchair before me, was somewhat surprised and equally disheartened when he learned that I was not in fact the patient, nor had I travelled all the way from England with the sole intention of making his acquaintance. I did, however, tell him every detail of my visit, omitting nothing, as instructed, no matter how apparently inconsequential.

About three hours later I concluded my account, while the Doctor, who was obviously affected by what he had heard, sitting, as he had throughout, impassively, in silence and growing more pallid by the minute, stared out blankly before him apparently deep in contemplation.

'Doctor?' I enquired, dreading that he may again have succumbed to another powerful reverie and failed to discern my entire narration.

'I need a drink,' he said firmly and motioned for my assistance to extricate him from the chair. After two unsuccessful attempts, he eventually managed to get to his feet and tottered off towards the bookshelves at the rear of the room, where he swung open a section of wall to reveal a well-stocked beverage cabinet and seized a cut glass decanter by the neck.

'You will join me?' he asked hospitably.

'Thank you,' I replied and was shortly presented with something akin to a small dry sherry, a pleasant though potent libation, and the Doctor topped a flagon of the same for himself. Returning to his seat, his colour amending to its former tone yet still appearing quite distraught by what I had told him, he sat quietly absorbed in his thoughts for some time before he spoke.

'Forgive me, Herr English, but what I have heard is most distressing. The past, it seems, has returned to haunt me. I knew the child's father. As boys we were the best of friends – inseparable in younger and happier days. Would you believe that we quarrelled in that very courtyard over twenty years ago? I have never been able to set foot out there since.

The Doctor then told the father's name but, for the life of me, I cannot remember what it was, although I think that it may have begun with the letter 'O' or perhaps 'G'.

'He married beneath him,' the Doctor continued, 'in a secret ceremony, conducted at midnight on the eve of All Saints' Day, to a common strumpet plucked from the woods during one of his many forays into the undergrowth. The family was horrified and cast him from its bosom, and he disappeared with his bride for several years but returned, the father of two young daughters, upon hearing that his last surviving relative had expired.

'On the night of his arrival, while celebrating the successful acquisition of his rightful inheritance, he was poisoned by an unknown assailant in the very room where you this day were forced to endure an odious plate of over-cured meat, questionable greens and, if I heard you correctly, a few measly under boiled potatoes. Naturally the waiter, a harmless simpleton, was pilloried for the crime, but I intervened at the behest of the town's clergy and had the boy released into my care, before the barbed steel and hot tongs were summoned and gingerly applied to his person, as is our custom. You have met him, I believe, his name is Carl and although he is not, as we say, the brightest iron in the fire, he is reasonably cheap and moderately trustworthy.

'As you may have gathered, Herr English, you are among a simple and superstitious people who will stop at nothing to oust evil from their lives – especially when they believe that it resides at their own door.

'Quickly, help me up!' he cried. 'We have not a moment to lose.'

The Doctor then left the room to prepare himself for the task ahead, and I remained to ponder the dubious nature of your dear brother's namesake who, on occasion and while grinning preposterously in my direction, would float in and out of the room in performance of a little light dusting.

Eventually, and most conveniently to my mind as I was finding the company decidedly uncomfortable, I heard a voice outside and swiftly moved through to the foyer where I found the Doctor standing resplendent in a pair of high-laced brown leather boots, a black fedora and corresponding cape.

'My bag,' he requested, and I handed him the article from the hallstand then waited patiently while he studiously examined the peculiar collection of instruments that were contained within. Having assured himself that everything was in order, he paused for a second by the plain mahogany framed wall mirror (a curious item that was awkwardly situated to the left of the front door) and then swept from the house with me fast on his coat tails.

The Doctor set a furious pace – covering over a yard with every stride – which I, at times, was at pains to replicate and even compelled to break into a light trot just to keep up. We sailed passed the police station, to the obvious astonishment of those inside who, as I observed through the large corner window, leapt to their feet spluttering mouthfuls of coffee at one another, while hurriedly donning the jackets and caps of their profession before hastening after us in the hottest possible pursuit.

We soon amassed quite a following and reached the hotel steps with retinue of about fifty of the town's most enquiring minds. Here the Doctor, relentless in his quest, flew ahead and crashed through the entrance where he hurdled the legs of the doorman, who had resumed his indolent repose and was subsequently overturned in his chair by those in the company of subordinate agility.

I managed to gain some ground on the Doctor and led him up the wide spiral staircase at the rear of the vestibule.

Incidentally, according to the hotel's receptionist, this wonderful example of traditional oak carving, vividly encompassing many exquisite details, is a unique feature of the building and regarded by many as a national treasure. The piece originates from the home of a wealthy landowner who commissioned the work in the late-17th century to commemorate the marriage of his burdensome daughter to Baron von (some-such-nonsense), a reserved gentleman of great sensibility who regrettably passed away on the night of the wedding at the grand old age of 102.

At the top of the stairs I introduced the Doctor to my quarters, with which he was less the impressed and had no desire to cross the threshold. I then directed him to the door of poor Helga's room, whereupon I was advised not to enter until he had made a thorough inspection of the scene for himself. The room had been cleaned and the body removed, but the Doctor was nevertheless most methodical in his explorations and I began to see him in quite another way, feeling that I had possibly misjudged his earlier eccentricities. He quietly and meticulously studied every point about him and meditatively drew upon his beard with each new encounter, while he pondered and deliberated his findings below his breath. The harmony of the inspection, however, was short lived and eventually consumed by many raised voices that were swiftly approaching from the corridor. I myself had considerable difficulty in preventing the room from being swamped by the Doctor's enthusiastic disciples, but the police constable and the hotel manager, who had squeezed to the fore, pressed their way into the room and were a great assistance to me in shutting the door against the spirited assembly outside.

The constable was furious and immediately

embarked upon a savage tirade of the Doctor, viciously chastising him for what he must have supposed was the discourteous invasion of his jurisdiction. The Doctor, however, was unperturbed and simply waited patiently until the constable had shouted himself into submission. He then turned to the constable and calmly whispered something into his ear. The constable replied with nothing, possibly because he was unable as he was now very short of breath, but he did managed to point to the floor, which seemed to indicate that what the Doctor sought was presently residing downstairs.

The Doctor dismissively ushered the constable aside and moved to the door, where he listened for a second then banged with his fist several times upon the panelling and bellowed out a single phrase in his native tongue. Silence was instantly restored and the Doctor, having regained his previous character, swung open the door and, like Moses dividing the waters of the Red Sea, walked serenely through crowd with the constable, the hotel manager and me following humbly behind. At the foot of the stairs we were forced to wait as the constable fumbled interminably with a large ring of keys, one of which would eventually allow us through the austere and diminutive door of the wine cellar.

The Doctor was first in, but the hotel manager remained close by with a small lantern to light the way. I entered after the constable and found much difficulty in descending the narrow wooden ladder in what was for me, bringing up the rear of our little expedition, almost complete darkness. I reached the bottom unable to see my hand before my face and sensed that I must be very far removed from the others, while deep within the cellar I could hear carpentry nails being drawn and the sound of breaking wood. Searching in my pockets I eventually found a match that I lit not an inch from the constable's nose, illuminating his astonished face and inadvertently scorching some of finer hairs of his moustache. I apologised, of course, but in my surprise I accidentally dropped the light, and again we were plunged into darkness – as the air was infused with the strong smell of burning. Unable to offer any further assistance, I could only listen in penitence as the constable nursed his pride and joy to the accompaniment of muffled groans, a sudden scream and at least one rack of wine bottles collapsing nearby. I moved away in all remorse – although mercifully unscathed – and delved further into the blackness with my arms outstretched before me.

In due course and keeping to the wall, I gradually rounded a corner to see in the distance the hotel manager's lantern and the silhouette of two men leaning over an open casket, which was raised from the ground on either side by two large wooden crates. I approached with all caution but respectfully waited some distance from the scene until the Doctor, with the most sombre expression, turned and beckoned me to advance further.

Nothing could have prepared me for the sight that I was about to witness, but do not distress yourself, my dearest, for it was not poor Helga, lying in her casket as pale as snow and the picture of serenity, who was about to astonish us all. Indeed, as we mournfully gazed upon this sweet innocent child in the soft ashen hue of the lantern, a black smoking spectre rose up from behind coffin, bleeding from the nose over the ruins of topiary, with a fearful bruise to the forehead and smelling dreadfully of alcohol. It was, of course, the police constable who, following his altercation with the wine rack and obviously disoriented, had crawled blind through the cellar and found his way to us by an alternative route. We then watched in dismay as this miserable being, still smouldering before us, casually extinguished himself with a bottle of house wine and straightened his dress as if nothing untoward had occurred.

'S-s-s-o,' he whistled courageously through a front tooth that was obviously troubling him, 'what is your opinion, Doctor?'

The Doctor nodded to the hotel manager, and the two men lifted the lid of the casket as though about to nail it shut.

'Herr Doctor, you do have an opinion, do you not?' asked the constable.

'I shall deliver my conclusions in due course,' returned the Doctor, but the constable was impetuous for answers.

'What do you say for the cause of death, Herr Doctor?'

The Doctor said nothing.

'How do you account the girl's pallid complexion?'

Again he did not reply, which made the constable

grow all the more impatient until, in a fit of temper that verged on insanity, he eventually demanded:

'What do you make of these two strange puncture marks on the victim's neck, Doctor Wagner?'

'Victim?' replied the Doctor calmly. 'You assume foul play is in evidence, yet I have seen nothing to indicate forced entry to the girl's room nor anything here to support your theory.'

'But Doctor, the marks,' barked the constable.

'Most intriguing. I must say that I have never seen anything like them in my entire life.'

'It looks like a bite of some sort,' suggested the constable. 'The girl has obviously been bitten by a wild animal during the night and the body drained of blood.'

'Nonsense,' replied the Doctor. 'Do not let your eyes see nor your ears hear that which you cannot account for. Ignorance is our worst enemy. No beast could ascend above the ground floor, nor gain entry to the girl's room with the window bolted from the inside. The main door was locked from within and the other impassable due to this gentleman's precautions and his wretched physical condition.'

I was beginning to like Doctor Wagner, in particular for his astute analytical mind, and I was honoured to assist both him and the hotel manager in replacing the lid of the casket while ignoring the additional protestations of the constable. I was also permitted to carry the Doctor's bag, and we returned to the hotel lobby where the Doctor pronounced before an expectant audience that the girl had unfortunately succumbed to an acute case of anaemia from spending too much time alone in her room with the shutters drawn, as was her practice. The insignificant marks on her neck were subsequently dismissed as the work of a particularly obstinate mosquito, a tenacious insect that is extremely common in the area during the spring months but entirely harmless.

There then followed much rejoicing and celebration, and the defenders of reason were showered with gratitude and great affection by all. I must confess I found the moment quite intoxicating and entirely incomparable, but the experience was short-lived and abruptly curtailed by a bloodcurdling scream from the hotel manager's wife who, in terror, was pointing at the cellar door before she fainted on the spot. There were more shrieks and gasps of fright as we all turned to watch the door slowly creak open – gripped by edge by a hideous blackened claw.

Our worst fears, however, were unfounded, for the gruesome visitation that appeared before us was none other than the hapless constable, who was returning dishevelled from his subterranean adventure and looking more than a little startled as he came out into the light.

Laughter abounded, and the constable was carried shoulder-high into the street, where he was thrown into the horse trough and, I later heard, out of his position of employment.

'Come,' hailed the Doctor, 'let us feast!' We then marched through to the dining-room with Doctor Wagner, the hotel manager and me at the front of a triumphant procession.

The evening proved a great success, and once more the hotel manager charged my glass time and again, although, with no intention of enacting the disgraceful lassitude of this morning, on several occasions I surreptitiously dispatched his offering into the earthenware pot of an adjacent geranium, not wishing to offend my host.

In the calmness of night, however, I now realise how insensitive I must have been as I recall, in a moment of heady delusion, asking if it would not be inconvenient to take advantage of the sizeable room that now lay unoccupied upstairs. I am honestly surprised that the hotel manager did not have me dragged from the building and horsewhipped for making such a suggestion, but he just shook his head and regrettably explained that he had already promised the room to his remaining stepdaughter who, as he put it, was ‘next in line’. I do not recall her name offhand, but I do remember that she was not at all enamoured by the prospect, although the hotel manager seemed more than adamant that the arrangement would proceed effectively.

Now, however, as I sit alone by the small mahogany writing table that occupies almost a quarter of my room, while the dizzy pleasures of the evening subside, I can only say that I must have been quite overcome by the evening’s festivities. My comprehension of what occurred must surely have been stifled by the giddy euphoria of the moment, while my ability to deduce anything of sense was undoubtedly swept away by the unabashed exuberance of those around me. I am sure that the events surrounding poor Helga's demise will never fully be realised as, and far be it from me to question the good Doctor's diagnosis, she did seem in the rudest of health when I last saw her.

I must end here for, in an effort to obtain at least one night's continual repose since my journey began, I have succumbed to the remainder of your dear mother's sleeping draft that I feel is now taking effect.

I will write again at the earliest opportunity, with any luck from the home of my client (with whom I look forward to meeting tomorrow) and which, I can only hope, is less exhilarating than here.

I am still missing you dreadfully, my dearest, but I am resolved that it is but a few short weeks before we shall be together again, and I remain confident that you will not falter nor weaken in my absence.

With all my love and thoughts,

Yours, as ever and always,

J.

Points of View

(in perspective)

She was beautiful. Magnificent. Mysterious. Perfection. The stuff of legends, books, dreams. Venus incarnate with the spirit of Helen and a smile by Leonardo. Majesty to behold, this vision of loveliness, this apparition that parts a crowd like a ship's prow gliding effortlessly through now familiar seas, a crew at ease and hold safe laden with bounteous returns, silently beating against the dawn.

A figurehead for all the female sex:/Sweet princess, 'shrined in awe 'twixt frail and thorn,/Of suitors lapping at her feet, doth seek,/From purest heart, the key that will unlock/Her own, yet mindful still, this queen of queens/To be, of match ill-proper from such stock.

Thy Goddess, no less, or that first image/Made, as if from marble hued, and given form that men might weep -

'What's the specky twat at the bar looking at, Sandra?'

Lost in t' Post

St Eaves: pleasant seaside resort on N Yorks coastline situated between Scarborough and Filey. Pop. 4122 (1951). Early closing Thu. Bustling in summer, dead in winter. Famed for 'St Eave's Crabs' – a local delicacy. Town named after Eave Glossop, loyal 'page' and confidante of Richard I. Born 1178, 'cruelly slain and her true sex revealed' (Rodger of Whitby, *Chronicles*, *c.* early-13th c.) 1192, during capture of king by Duke Leopold V on return from Holy Land. Glossop canonised 1242, but sainthood annulled by Vatican when Durham University professor on cycling tour of Austria provides 'irrefutable evidence Glossop none other than Eve "Penny" Godling, notorious "Whitby Whore" and instigator of dubious yet highly profitable 12th-c. enterprise that flourished throughout northern England' (Prof. G.H. Crozier, *Telegram to Dean Grantham*, Jul. 23, 1911).

Wed., Feb. 6, 1952: Afternoon; cloud over St Eave's Mount, breezy down to bay, light rain; town deserted.

Althorp, Margaret Ann: Born: Aug. 13, 1918. Marital status: single. Education: Denby Dale School for Infants 1923-9, Linthwaite Seniors 1929-33. Qualifications: 11+. Previous employment: Bracket's Mill, Huddersfield 1933-9, WVS 1939-45. Character: diligent with cheerful disposition. Post: Assistant Librarian.

'Margaret/Maggie/Mags'. Big bones, ebony hair tied in bun, round face hidden behind thick rimmed spectacles, dark brown eyes, prominent brows (slight down on upper lip); plain yellow headscarf, flat shoes for comfort; disposition beginning to wane.

Usual raincoat, usual hurry. Shop bell of Hackett & Sons clanging to action – just in time. Loyal Jake slumbering in sawdust by open fire. 'Couple o' eggs for breakfast and what meat rations will allow.'

Out again, past Ted's Café, miniature golf and trampolines – all closed. Through park, along by rhododendrons, bandstand, boating lake, swings and drained paddling pool – not a soul in sight. On again, along street, up lane, round corner, 'Terrible weather Mrs Whitcomb.' Home.

Bed and Breakfast (seasonal Apr. 1-Sep. 30): Two rooms plus dining/lounge. Hot water 6am-8.30am. Soap 2d., towels 1d. each. Wireless 7pm-9pm. Close to bus terminus and beach; pleasant ambiance, sea views. 26 Motley Crescent, St Eaves.

Voices in kitchen. Dad and... others? Other. Male, loud, raucous. (Quickly, quietly, come back later.) Carefully – too late.

''Ave thee enough theer for company, Maggie?'

Squeezing round door that opens wrong way swinging string bags of groceries, puffing, straining, sweating. 'Dad? Oh, I'm sorry,' backing out again, 'I didn't realise you were entertaining.'

'Terrible bashful is our Mags. Allow me to make introductions. Maggie Althorp, mah daughter an' woman o' t' 'ouse; Teddy Granger, scholar, sportsman an' man o' t' world to boot.'

Granger, Edward George: (alias 'Ted Granger, Teddy Grange, Dr Edward Strange, Rev. George Stranger'.) Last known address: no fixed abode. Age: 50(ish). Height: 5'11". Build: portly. Distinguishing features: balding pate, amply freckled, occasional RAF handlebar moustache (ginger). Wanted in connection with allegations concerning several cases of obtaining monies by deception.

This week: 'Teddy Granger'. Sitting legs astride, chaffing palms; tweed jacket (patched at elbows), cream nylon shirt (fraying at sleeves), red and white poker dot bow tie, grey flannels creased down length, brown brogues – slightly muddy but otherwise buffed to a high sheen, camelhair overcoat and small battered leather case on knees.

Uprooting unsuccessful. Planting as before, puffing by stove. Dad wheezing beside, grinning.

Althorp, Ernest Arthur: GPO employee no. 2814/B. Mar. 1, 1948. District: St Eaves Central. Remarks: reasonably punctual.

'Ah met Ted on mah round, luv. A real character 'e is – once thee gets to know 'im, once thee cuts through yon dapper exterior. Eh, Ted? 'Ave thee in stitches afore long 'e shall – wi' 'is wry jokes an' 'is witty asides an' what 'ave thee. Been telling me all about 'imself an' 'is latest adventures. That's t' sole purveyor o' most durable female undergarments this side o' t' Dales sitting theer afore thee, ah'll 'ave thee know. Thee could learn a thing or two off this fella, Mags. Eh? Ah'd say. A good man in a crisis, if thee asks me.

Eh, Ted?' Asthmatic laughing. 'A good man in a crisis.' More of the same.

Approaching cautiously making apologies for Dad, etc., can be a bit crude at times.

'Pleased to meet you, Mr Granger.'

Another standing effort hopelessly ineffectual. Hands finally clasping, grasping, slipping, sweating – never more awkward.

'Oh, I say, do call me Teddy. Teddy Granger, that's me. And if I may be so bold as to call you Margaret? Your father's told me all about you, the pleasure's mine.'

Stuffing pipe bowl from opened pouch, 'We don't stand on ceremony 'ere, do we, Maggie? Lot o' bloody nonsense! Thee'll find none airs an' graces in this 'ouse, Ted – make no mistake.'

Maggie smiling, trembling, peeling out of raincoat, rolling sleeves, hauling pan on stove. Occasionally making shy glances over chopped vegetables, always finding Ted's eyes rooted above idiotic paralysed smile. Dad observing, beaming absurdly.

'Aye, so... stuck for digs then, are thee?'

'Well, yes actually. Damnable hearing about that Railway Inn, pardon my French.'

Through ochre stained teeth gripping chipped pipe stem, 'Maggie can air one o' yon upstairs rooms after tea. Wouldn't put thee out on a night like this – what wi' 'otel closed out o' t' season anall. 'Ave we spare doings for Ted staying t' night, Mags?'

Without looking up, 'I'm sure I'll manage somehow.'

Unnerving pause.

'Well now, see here, if I'm in anyway imposing or, or, or what have you, I'd just as soon -'

Dad stretching out legs from chair, surreptitiously reassuring Ted she'll come round eventually.

'It's only Monday's broth I'm afraid. I just keep adding to it each day.' On closer inspection, 'Should really start from scratch.'

'Smells delicious.'

'She's a treasure to me that one, Ted. A real treasure to me, she is.'

'Well, I must say, this is awfully good of you both. I'd have been in a real jam if I hadn't run into you as I did, Ernest.'

'Think nothing o' it, Ted.'

'No, I mean, really. You wouldn't believe this, Margaret, and honestly I don't usually go into these places, but as luck would have it your father here -'

Sudden coughing fit, artificially violent, by Dad desperately trying to change subject.

'Yes, well, jolly decent of you both, I say. Damn good show, what? Pardon my French again.'

'Least we can do' (for buying him unlawful drink in Godling Arms all afternoon). Maggie seeing right through this one – straight to core.

Another nervous hush.

'I say, isn't this weather awful? Mm? Neither one thing nor the other, is it? Can't quite seem to make up its mind what it wants to be.'

'It's been like this all week, Mr Granger.'

'Oh, has it really? Still, soon be spring, eh? And

then summer. I'm sure this is quite the place to be in summer. Jolly nice I'd imagine.'

'It were a scorcher up 'ere last year, Ted.'

'Really?'

'A reet scorcher! August bank 'oliday were 'ottest. Ah were out t' back in nowt but me smalls – soaking it up ah were. Very pleasant. Very agreeable ah found it. O' course, doesn't suit our Maggie.'

'No?'

'Comes out in 'ives in t' sun she does, don't thee, Mags?'

'Ives?'

'Aye, 'ives. Great 'ives. 'Ives all over.'

'Oh, hives!'

''Ives, aye. 'As to stay indoors. Keep 'erself covered up in t' sun. Stay in t' shade.'

'That's a pity.'

'Not like me. An' Stan! Ah'll tell thee, Ted – when our Stanley came 'ome from Burma 'e looked like a ruddy sambo.'

no. 241 Althorp, Stanley Ernest: Sgt-Maj, DSO. 2nd Bn, King's Own Yorkshire Light Infantry: Mar. '33. POW Rangoon: May '42-Aug. '45. MEDICAL DISCHARGE: Sep. '45. Admitted Huddersfield Royal Infirmary: Feb. 24, '46. Transferred Summerfield Lodge, Home for Ex-Servicemen, Meltham: Mar. 3, '47-Apr. 18, '47.

Stan by curtains in old room again – just as before but unable to sit still for five minutes. Constantly pacing. Palpitations. Vigilantly peering out window into faint strip of light. Sadistic cries and laughter in street below. Monotonous children's song chanting in head like foreign language. Same thing over and over...

Night. Nothing to worry about now, not in jungle anymore. Brief relapse from sickness. Sudden uproar, lights, panic, screaming. Dragged from bed face down by ankles strapped to bamboo pole. Hauled from sickbay onto parade ground, hands and face splashing in freshly spilt blood of cheery Col. Chilton pooling under severed head. Same fate awaiting Dennis Bagley, last but one of Black Hand gang, on his knees behind. Burning pain on soles of feet eventually becoming numb.

Six weeks cramped with dying, starving with fever in darkness and heat.

'Aye, t' sun never troubled our Stanley.'

'Blessed onions!' Maggie stepping outside for a moment.

'Just need a breath of fresh air, that's all.' Muffled sobs in back yard.

'Look here, Ernest, are you sure this is such a good idea? Old Mags there seems a bit put out with me.'

'Don't thee worry, Ted. 'As 'er moods now an' again – women's... whatnots. Nothing to concern thee. She'll come round soon enough.'

'Well, it's a bit bloody awkward.'

Ernest undeterred. Maggie returning in silence. Broth sloping into two bowls on kitchen table. Rhubarb and custard following.

Men creeping diffidently forward.

'I say, not eating?'

‘Keeping an eye on ’er figure, aren’t thee, luv?’ Aside to Ted but not far enough, ‘Just as well, none other bugger will.’ Asthmatic laughter.

‘Oh, I’m... sure that isn’t true.’

Silence.

Nervous converse throughout, never really getting off ground.

‘Have you always lived in the area?’

Knowing glances.

‘Is Mrs Althorp still... Ah, pity.’

Furious slurping from Dad’s end of table.

‘And what do you do Margaret? Is it rewarding? I like a good detective story myself. Have you read any Margery Allingham? She’s awfully good. Awfully clever I always think. What’s the name of that man of hers called? Camp... Champ... something or other.’

‘Campion.’

‘That’s the fellow! Albert Campion. Doesn’t miss a trick, does he? What was the last one of hers I remember? *More Work for the Undertaker*. Didn’t think much of that. *Traitor’s Purse* is my favourite. Have you read it?’

Allingham, Margery Louise: 1904 -. *Traitor’s Purse*, (William Heinemann: London, Toronto, 1941, 8o, Crime/Adult Fiction. NN.32288.

‘Yes, well... damn silly really – if you’ll pardon my French.’

‘She’s a deep one is our Maggie. Reet scholarly, ah says. Always got ’er nose in a book, she ’as.’

‘Well, I should imagine that’s jolly useful if you work in a library, wouldn’t you think? Jolly useful indeed, I'd say. All alphabetical I expect these days, is it?'

Smiling, nodding politely, 'I'll put the kettle on, shall I?'

Ted sitting most uncomfortably, drawing enormous white handkerchief from trouser pocket and mopping perspiration from brow to back of neck.

'Warm enough theer are thee, Ted?' Breathless chuckles. 'Thee could ring that out to dry.' More hysterical convulsions drowned out by ferocious but timely filling of kettle.

Silent stillness. Ted holding teacup and saucer, side plate of crumbs balancing on knee, stirring thin air. Maggie darning stockings. Dad fast asleep driving home snores.

'We usually have wireless on about this time, Mr Granger, but it means warming up front room.'

'Oh, please, don't trouble yourself on my account. I'm very comfortable here, thank you. Very comfortable.'

More embarrassing deliveries.

'Yes, this is a pleasant room, isn't it?' Courteously admiring décor (with particular eye for any profitable items, unable to suppress habit of a lifetime). 'Jolly nice display of picture postcards. Charming. Hobby of some sort?'

'More tea, Mr Granger?'

'Well, only if -'

'I'll make a fresh pot.'

Dad surfacing thinking he's losing track of time. Up wooden hill to Bedfordshire. Ted sitting forward perspiring in anxious posture with second cup drained, wanting to speak... everything to say but unable to utter a word. Time racing past – or standing still. Dreadful silence.

Maggie watching cautiously from behind sewing.

Head down, sweating, eyes burning, rocking to and fro muttering something to himself.

'Mr Granger.'

More absurd ramblings.

'Are you well, Mr Granger?'

Advancing guardedly, 'Mr Granger?' Placing affectionate hand on shoulder. 'Teddy?'

'Eh? What? Who? Oh, sorry.'

'Are you alright.'

'Absolutely! Never better. Teddy Granger, that's me!'

'You seemed to drift off there for a moment.'

'Did I? How silly.'

'Can I get you anything?'

'No, really, I'm perfectly well, thank you. Perfectly... Yes. I have these odd... you know, from time to time. Get a bit light-headed. Feel a bit woozy – usually when I'm not doing anything. Can't sort of... settle for any length of time. Seem to... I'm fine if I'm busy, on the move and what have you, but when I... Oh, I do say, that was quite a turn, wasn't it?'

'Perhaps I should fetch the doctor?'

'No, no, please, no doctors. I'll be alright in a moment. Need to take a few deep breaths – that usually does the trick. Be right as rain in no time... if I just... If only I...'

Hours later. Ted in disarray, about to get rid of something he's been carrying for a very long time.

'The thing is, Maggie, to be perfectly frank with you, I'm... a bit of a sham really. Just some... damn... bloody fraud, if truth be told, pardon my French. Not what you see at all. It's a sort of act. Always has been, come to think of it. Never spoken like this to anyone before – gift of the gab and all that rot. I'm one of those blokes they say can... charm the birds from the trees, you know?' Raising a smile. 'Sell snow to the Eskimos.' Laughing. 'Sand to the Arabs, that's me! It's only when one... stops and thinks for a moment... it all suddenly catches up with one. The past, I mean, plays tricks with the mind sometimes, wouldn't you say? Especially when one's... tired... been on the road a while. Should really think about settling down somewhere... one of these days. Somewhere quiet. Peaceful. Perhaps even find myself a... Oh, I say, you must think me a awful prune sitting here like this, getting all sentimental and what have you. I must apologise, really I must. I'm sure its just... '

Lame excuses fading out with Maggie sheering through dapper exterior, intently studying perfect soulmate.

'Yes, well... enough of all that nonsense. I say, look at the time. Gracious me! Second on the left did you say? Best be off then. Goodnight.'

'Sleep well, Ted.'

Maggie alone again but never more content listening to kitchen clock ticking on wall.

Other significant events of the day: King George VI

dies of cancer at Sandringham aged 56. Succeeded by eldest daughter Elizabeth.

Thu., Feb. 7, 1952: 8.20am. Dad scrutinizing morning paper over cooked breakfast halfway through round. Maggie bringing on seconds from frying pan.

'End o' an era. Eh, luv?'

'Aye.'

'Ted up yet?'

'Nope.'

'Ah thought ah 'eard 'im call out or summit in t' night. 'Ellish blood-curdling it were, did thee 'ear? Ah must 'ave been dreaming. What do thee make o' 'im, Maggie? Funny bloke, ah reckon. Quite a character 'e is, all t' same. Honest as t' day's long, mind, thee can't deny that.'

Mid-morning. House quiet again. Still no sign of Ted but paper missing from hallstand.

Maggie crawling up stairs. Listening at bedroom door second on left. Retreating quietly. Returning following judicious interval.

'Mr Granger.' Another modest tap. 'It's almost eleven, Mr Granger.' Cautiously reaching for handle, sticking head round opening door, 'Mr Granger?'

Coated figure by window leaning on sill, looking fearfully out through misty sky towards coast – reminiscent of Stan back in Huddersfield.

'Ted?' Slowly drawing level with comparable unease.

'What's the trouble, Ted?'

Turning to face her in obvious distress, 'Maggie!' Hand on cheek. Hand on hand, eyes closing in response. Holding, pressing. Years of waiting, hoping, longing, falling away, forgotten. A single moment lasting always. Life is real again.

'I don't remember when I last... the last time I... '

Shrill blast from steam whistle approaching St Eave's Station on south-bound line.

Ted careering down stairs, regrettably committing to urgent business but promising to write soon.

Halting at front door with renewed spring in step. Maggie, breathless as a schoolgirl from parting kiss, shamelessly waving up street in spite of neighbours.

Letter box springing hopefully to life with door closing behind new woman.

'Dear Ernest and Margaret': Black and white. 'Harbour, Bridlington' (*c.* 1910), 6"x4", Anon.

Dad handing over morning post between mouthfuls at breakfast table. (Innocent enough. All open and above board. Nothing to worry about... yet.)

Many thanks for hospitable accommodation. Never forget kindness of St Eave's good Samaritans. Thought Maggie might like postcard for collection. Not terribly inspiring but apparently jolly historic. Here 3 days, pressing on Monday.

Sincerely yours,

Teddy Granger.

''E gets about, doesn't 'e? Eh? Always on t' move that one. Always restless, did thee notice? 'E were reet restless. Must be some sort o' nervous disposition 'e's got. Same as our Stan, I expect. 'E were like that towards t' end.'

Frying pan slamming on stove, likewise kitchen door in frame, enough to wake dead. Stiffened snivels in back yard.

Cathedral of St Peter, York: West Front; dusk. 'Choirboys heading for evensong', photographed by Mr Francis Hawkins RPS.

Dear Margaret,

Couldn't resist this one. Spotted in little tobacconists near Shambles – immediately thought of you. Once again, every thanks for kindness and generosity. Regards to Ernest.

With all best wishes,

Ted.

'"With all best wishes" now then, is it? Thee must o' made quite an impression on that lad, eh? To 'ave 'im splash out on picture postcards – festooned wi' God knows what kind o' fancy talk an' what 'ave thee. Where's all this leading, ah'd very much like to know? Ah've every right to know what mah daughter's been getting up to behind mah back. Tha's started t' neighbours chattering already, ah've noticed – wi' thi shameless public displays. Oh aye, ah've 'eard about thee an' 'im canoodling in middle o' t' street for all t' world to see. Bloody disgraceful at thi time o' life, that is. Not natural, is it? Not natural at all, ah say. An' ah'll tell thee another thing afore thee go, ah don't bloody trust 'im neether! Ah've met 'is sort afore – all laughs an' jokes one minute, t' next thee'll be standing in nowt but thi bloody draws, if 'e 'asn't 'ad them off thee already.'

Maggie alone in yard facing cold morning breeze, stupidly letting all heat out of house.

Rooms for Gentlemen: Pleasant lodgings in quiet suburban residence. Weekly/monthly lettings. Competitive rates. Proprietor: Mrs J. Collier, Rosewood House, Queen's Way, Holbeck.

'Mm, jolly nice, thank you Mrs Collier. Jolly comfortable indeed. Yes... just the job! Now then, I shall be taking the room for about three weeks or so – tying up a few loose ends and what have you, clearing the decks, so to speak – then bashing off probably around the beginning of March if things work out. Going to making a fresh start in the spring, possibly abroad somewhere.'

'That's entirely satisfactory with me, Mr Granger. Perfectly affable, wholly acceptable and thoroughly conducive with my arrangements. 'Ave thee got summit else lined up for thisen?'

'Well, I am rather hoping to get married actually, Mrs Collier.'

'To Miss Margaret Althorp': More flowery notepaper; same jocular tone, harmless small talk mostly but requesting reply now settled at new address. Ominous 'xxx' and 'T.G.' on reverse of 'River Aire at Dawn' enclosed.

Dad in snug of Godling Arms draining modest but well-earned refreshment, straining bleary eyed through pipe smoke to read.

Brief flash in coal fire beside, dying to resume faint glow. Disparaging glances returning to bar.

'Dearest Margaret/Dear Maggie/My Darling Maggie/Beloved Mags... ' **Dear Maggie**: Leeds postmark, excessive postage.

Dad sliding envelope from inside pocket of overcoat behind kitchen door – right under Maggie's nose.

'Ah'll be off then, Mags.'

'Aye, I'll just finish up a few things here first.'

'As thee wish.'

Dad scurrying up wooden hill. Soon quietly perusing numbered pages at leisure, written by candlelight on rickety table in jolly comfortable room of respectable Leeds boarding house.

Ted cutting to chase, finally doing away with all that lovey-dovey chit-chat. Dad's eyes darting over compelling sentiments of undeniable honesty: '... no saint... many regrets... not proud of... past... pressures... meeting you... kindness... love... must leave... away urgently... Continent... Saturday... station... 4pm... new life... always... together... love... lots of love... '

Mon., Jun. 2, 1953: Late evening; fine and warm. Riotous celebrations in High Street.

Bed and Breakfast: Closed until weekend due to bereavement.

Maggie in overalls and turban listening to wireless having just got house back to normal.

Popping upstairs into cleared back room for one last look before decorators move in. Four yellow stained walls, except where pictures were hung, definitely wanting smartening up; naked bulb dangling from ceiling, bare boards marking where awful carpet once lay – one loose under foot.

Maggie on knees lifting stubborn floorboard, finally removing bundle of dusty envelopes obstructing below.

no. 1382 Granger, Edward George.

'The Fraudster'. Sitting in darkness on wire framed bed with chamber pot at feet, concluding first anniversary of exemplary sentence.

Other significant events of the day: Coronation of Queen Elizabeth II at Westminster Abby, London.

Bed and Breakfast: Vacancies. Three rooms plus dining/lounge...

5.40 JESSICA *'Shape Up or Ship Out!'*

6.00 DOT-COM HIGH (*Omnibus*)

Petals is faced with a moral dilemma, while Snoopy learns an important lesson in life.

6.30 SOLAR POWER (*New Series*)

Yes it really is that time of year again! So, blow up the beach ball and dig out the deckchairs. Fun in the sun from Margate to Majorca.

7.00 ROUND THE HOUSES

Classic comedy (*rpt*)

7.30 STIR CRAZY (*New*)

Hot-foot from his successful afternoon game show *Rattle Those Pots and Pans*, top 'dish' Adrian Bellows discovers a 16th-century recipe for mince, resurrects the humble artichoke for a celebrity banquet and meets an Ulster poulterer on his quest for the perfect omelette.

8.00 ELIXIR

Six more contestants compete for the ultimate prize.

8.30 SOILED

Horticultural hilarity.

9.00 EDEN PLACE *Trouble in Paradise*

Molly is in a spin over daughter Jude's dress sense, Deirdre has more doubts about the wedding, and negotiations with council officials reach stalemate in the on-going saga of Ted's allotment.

9.40 RIP IT OUT AND START AGAIN
More radical home makeovers from the team that brought you *Would You Look at the State of This Place* and *Those Curtains Will Have to Go For a Start!*

10.00 REPEAT PRESCRIPTION
For Emergencies Only
Cash crises in casualty.

11.00 SINGLES *The Game Goes On*
Chloe is hoping for a proposal, while Beverley and the girls continue their search for 'Mr Right'.

11.45 FULCRUM
Topical debate with an invited audience from Belfast.

12.45 WORLD'S MOST GRUESOME CRIMES – EVER! 3

1.45 SUDS
Preview of the week's soaps.

2.15 RENAISSANCE WOMEN *Should Prostitution be Legalised?*

3.00 PROVED BEYOND DOUBT *Reincarnation*

3.30 SEX! SEX! SEX!
Forthright discussion about 'you know what', plus candid dramatisations of the real thing.

4.00 THOSE GLORY, GLORY DAYS
England v Germany
Re-live all the action from the 1966 World Cup final.

5.40 JESSICA (*rpt*)

The Final Chapter

On April 6, 1971, a small item appeared in the *Torbay Evening Enquirer* announcing that an unidentified elderly woman had been knocked down by a motorcycle in the centre of Torquay. The women is said to have been 'unconscious but in a stable condition at Torbay Hospital', while police were still searching for the rider who, it is reported, 'had callously remounted and sped from the scene'.

Initial efforts to identify the woman were unsuccessful, but later that evening staff nurse Martin Brady, who was arriving for night duty, immediately recognised her from a faded photograph, taken several years before, on the back cover of a dog-eared paperback in the hospital's reception area. Brady was particularly drawn to the tiny port-wine stain in the shape of a pair of hanging scales just below the woman's right eye and which, regardless of any efforts to conceal the blemish, was still visible in the publicity photograph. The book, entitled *Death in the Desert* (1924), was the first and least successful of an otherwise flawless series of detective novels to feature the flamboyant amateur sleuth Crichton Gable, while its author is perhaps one of the most popular crime writers of the 20th century.

Cicely Carrington, or 'C.C.' as she was known to her friends and loyal readership, was born on St

George's Day, 1890, at the family home of Oakfield near Paignton in Torbay. Her father was Godfrey Alexander Carrington, a brash American who derived a substantial income from several obscure business dealings in New York. Her mother, Eva Agnes Carrington, came from the fashionable St Austell Galloways and was a founding member of the Women's Social and Political Union. Eva Carrington was rumoured to have been among those responsible for ascending Nelson's Column and painting the statue pink on the 100th anniversary of the Battle of Trafalgar, although nothing was ever proved and she always vehemently denied any involvement in the stunt. The remaining family consisted of an older sister Merle, to whom Cicely was devoted, and two younger brothers, Godfrey and Maurice or 'Little Mo' as he was perpetually called. Unlike Merle, who attended Roedean, Cicely was considered too delicate for the rough and tumble of a traditional boarding-school education and was therefore taught at home by her mother and a succession of governesses.

As the sun set on the Victorian era the Carrington's hectic social and seasonal engagements continued at a relentless pace, while for Cicely, who is said to have been 'an impressionable gal from the off' (Audrey Homes, *Domestic Bliss: The Exploits of an English Nanny*, 1948), life at Oakfield must have seemed like one giddy turn of whimsical pleasure after another. Her affluent and sheltered upbringing also allowed Cicely to concentrate her efforts on the conventional pastimes of young women, however, in 1903, following the death of Godfrey Carrington, a traditionalist and staunch Republican, Eva Carrington threw herself into campaigning and was perhaps influential in nurturing Cicely's early interest in politics. In a poem, possibly inspired by her mother's demonstrations and later published in the freethinking and occasionally scandalous *Plymouth Tribune* (Dec. 6, 1918), the 13-year-old Cicely writes:

> The day we see is a day unplanned,
> Hour upon hour is the hour we stand;
> A minute lost, as time unfolds,
> Is a minute gained by the upper hand.
>
> 'Equivalence' (1904)

Cicely was never an active participant in the movement, although during her teenage years she did write at length on the subject with a view to publication. However, in the summer of 1912, Cicely was introduced to Wilfred Blancheford, the son of the influential Conservative MP Maxwell Blancheford, and the project was abandoned shortly after. The couple were married on June 7, 1913, and took up residence at Oakfield where life now assumed a more sedate pace. Eve Carrington desisted from any further political activities and confined herself to a single attic room in the family home, until she died of tuberculosis in September the same year. The Blanchefords still entertained, but the outbreak of war in August 1914 severely curtailed the social calendar. Wilfred went straight to France where he distinguished himself to receive the CMG but never returned. Cicely, meanwhile, became a nurse with the Voluntary Aid Detachment in Torquay, during which time she worked in the dispensary where she undoubtedly acquired her extensive knowledge of poisons.

The years after the war were uneventful for Cicely and she began to adopt a reclusive existence at Oakfield, while the interest on debts accrued in her name by the late Colonel Blancheford mounted intolerably.

In July 1922, however, while attending a summer fête at Newton Abbot, Cicely encountered the Rev. Harold Stevens who immediately became a close friend and companion. Rev. Stevens was nearly 20 years her senior and, having secured himself as vicar of the nearby St Mary's, became a regular houseguest at Oakfield. In the following year Cicely and the reverend toured Egypt together where, through a heated argument and a chance remark over dinner, Cicely began formulating the idea for her first book. The setting is based on an isolated archaeological dig three days' drive from Cairo, which Cicely and the reverend visited on several occasions, while the character of Crichton Gable is thought to have been inspired by the jocular variety entertainer Freddy Fopps who was staying at the same hotel. The manuscript was published under her maiden name, and although *Death in the Desert* is praised by one critic as 'a demonstration of exceptional originality' (J.P. Harrison, *Manchester Post*, Jun. 27, 1924), the book was a financial disaster, and Cicely was required to produce a further six novels before Oakfield was secured.

During this period, with Cicely seated at her typewriter for up to 14 hours a day, the Rev. Stevens was engaged on work of his own. He had already put aside his *Complete History of the Civilized World*, a colossal and heroic undertaking that was never completed, in favour of the universally popular *Under the Stairs* books, 'a series of stories about an amiable young lad named Jonathan Foster who surreptitiously introduces London street urchins to a life of merry subservience in Belgravia' (Rev. Stevens, *Letter to the Commissioning Editor, Huffa-Puffa Books Ltd*, Feb. 8, 1925). Rev. Stevens also wrote extensively about his earlier career with the Royal Navy, although, at a time when bookshops were awash with memoirs of the Great War, the reverend's modest efforts about life as a petty officer in Plymouth were unfortunately swamped by more sensational titles.

In March 1926, Cicely's third book, *Vengeance for Padre Phipps*, was completed and the formula for each successive novel was perfected – although, in an effort to maintain continuity, readers are often asked to suspend disbelief with what occasionally verges on the incredible. There is always the mysterious death, the closed circle of suspects, each with a motive and opportunity to commit the crime, and at the centre, like some bizarre ringmaster officiating over a macabre circus, the astonishing figure of Crichton Gable with his incomparable powers of logical deduction.

The settings and players vary considerably from the

Parisian adventure of *Murder on the Metro* (1928) to the drive for power and riches by master criminals in *Parliamentary Questions* (1930). Yet the form never deviates from the classical detective story and is the blueprint for most subsequent crime fiction. Simply, it is an enigma that begins with a single undeniable fact: a murder. The form then broadens (or, as they say, the plot thickens) as the investigation develops, and then, like a geometrical construction, it will narrow abruptly towards the end – upon another single undeniable fact: the murderer.

The character of Crichton Gable is equally resolute and alters little from his original conception in *Death in the Desert*, where an obscure figure descends upon the company having carelessly found himself detached from the Bedouin caravan with which he was travelling. The passage not only assures Crichton Gable's inalienable position in literary history, but also introduces the reader to a unique and extraordinary figure whose background, like the desert from which he has walked, is totally obscure.

> Abigail looked up over the body of dearly departed Edgar as her tears dried swiftly in the afternoon sun.
>
> Dr Stedman led her aside to be comforted by the others, and he ordered the natives to remove the deceased to his tent where he would conduct a thorough examination for himself.
>
> Not that there was any doubt as to what had killed poor Edgar. Remorse for his past

misdemeanours had certainly weighed heavy upon him at dinner the previous evening, and, in their separate locations, each member of Prof. Harrington's excavation party had heard the single gunshot, downed tools and immediately rushed to the spot where Sir Algernon's eldest son lay resolutely clasping Hugo von Braun's smoking revolver in his left hand. He had also shown more than a passing interest in where the German chose to conceal his weapon, and the former Oxford sculls champion was further witnessed by Lady Cuthbert sobbing uncontrollably to himself that morning.

Following Dr Stedman's extensive evaluation, which, in keeping with his usual professionalism, lasted a thorough twenty minutes, the physician finally threw open the tent flap and appeared before the company sombrely wiping his arms with a blood-stained hand towel.

'He must have shot himself for some reason,' deduced the doctor, and they all adjourned to the shade of the awning where Dawson and precious Ali had again surpassed themselves (although not without the occasional disagreement) in the preparation of afternoon tea.

About an hour later, while they all mused philosophically over Edgar's departure and even poor Abigail had resigned herself to returning the couple's plentiful wedding gifts, von Braun sat up from his semi-recumbent posture to notice a curious spectacle on the horizon. He observed the phenomenon for several minutes before cautioning the others, and each, in turn but no less confounded, regarded the advancing apparition with equal consternation.

It was a man. He came from the east but might just as well have tumbled from the sky.

He was dressed in brightly coloured clothes and carried a parasol, while his nonchalant perambulation in one of the most inhospitable environs imaginable resembled a quiet Sunday stroll in the park. He may even have walked straight through the camp had Dr Stedman not confronted the stranger and requested his name and business.

With the notable exception of *Gable's Folly* (1956), in which the usually reserved hero allows himself to become romantically entangled with the manipulative Madame d'Orsay, Gable remains a remote and ambiguous figure whose undying loyalty to 'the bright young things' with whom he benevolently associates never wavers.

Throughout the fiction speculation abounds as to his previous exploits, and suggestion of his origins reaches fever pitch in *All the King's Men* (1932) when Captain Dawlish jokingly implies that he might even be the illegitimate son of Edward VII. There are also rumours of secret drinking, a debilitating opium addiction, soaring gambling debts and a string of loose women in demand of hush money, but none of these foibles ever come to fruition, nor are they explored beyond the realms of idle gossip.

Although Gable is regularly teased and hoodwinked by the aristocratic practical joker Shamus O'Casey, with whom there are many notable spats, his worst enemy is perhaps himself, riddled as he is by reserved feelings of self doubt, underachievement and acute loneliness. The memorable retort by the young Marquis of Highborn aboard ship in *Murder Afloat* (1950) bluntly illustrates Gable's ability to conclude an inquiry with his customary flair and to everyone's delight, while still failing to ingratiate himself with the company.

> Gable slumped back into the captain's chair, with which he had made bold throughout his summation, as the fiendish Hungarian was led away by the master-at-arms with triumphant applause for the great detective ranging petulantly in his ears.
>
> 'Yes, yes. Jolly clever, Gable,' congratulated Dudley as the ovation subsided. 'Now look here, everyone – who's for quoits?'

In 1928, following the discovery of her Austin Seven lying abandoned near Hastings, Cicely became the subject of her own mystery when she famously 'vanished from the public gaze during a strenuous but, for the most part, highly successful three week publicity tour along the south coast of England' (*Daily Herald*, Jul. 25, 1928). The story was headline news and much of the national press championed all efforts to locate the missing novelists. One newspaper was soon to offer '£200 reward for information leading to the discovery of Mrs Blancheford' while displaying several photographs of Cicely 'as she might appear if disguised by altering the style of her hairdressing and wearing glasses' (*Graphical Mail*, Jul. 28, 1928).

As the search entered its second week, with the coastline and surrounding countryside having been scoured in vain by hundreds of police officers, Boy Scouts and thousands of enthusiastic members of the public, speculation on the case mounted unremittingly, and all details, both pertinent and otherwise, were immediately consumed by the insatiable appetite of the press. Great excitement abounded with the discovery of a pillbox hat, thought to have belonged to the absent writer, that was found in the hedgerow by the side of a country road on the outskirts of Chichester. As attention moved to the South Downs the item was handed over to the renowned clairvoyant Edna Gabble, who made the startling prediction that '"the hat's owner is lying dead several miles from the spot where it was found"' (*Times Newspaper*, Jul. 31, 1928).

Mercifully no body materialised, but a middle aged woman by the name of Mrs Irene Roper eventually admitted ownership of the hat, which had been gifted to her by an unwelcome admirer and thrown from her speeding car. Mr Arthur Priestly of Worthing immediately recognised his discarded and weather-damaged bequest from a photograph in his morning newspaper, which, to his astonishment, he found prominently displaying the aforementioned article and Miss Gabble strenuously pondering its significance.

Distinguished public figures were also invited to offer their opinion on the case, while daily reports in the press would often proclaim 'Fresh Developments', yet closer inspection of the text invariably revealed nothing new. Under the blaring headline '"C.C." ABDUCTED BY BOLSHEVIKS' (*Evening Echo* Aug. 1, 1928), the popular radio broadcaster and wit Cornelius Wincanton says that he was 'once lured into an alleyway in Folkestone by a suspicious looking character with a Russian accent and one of those black fluffy hats that they wear'. Wincanton goes on to describe the occasion in great detail, but it eventually transpires that the gentleman in question was only interested in obtaining a cheap ticket to the Continent.

All this time, however, Cicely remained oblivious to the mounting hysteria as, apparently exhausted by the arduous itinerary set by her publisher, she had retreated to an isolated location in Dorset with the Rev. Stevens, who owned a small property on the coast.

Cicely's car had simply run out of petrol, a fact that was never spotted by journalists nor the police, while the novelist maintained that she had always intended to retrieve the vehicle at a later date.

The couple returned to Oakfield and the inevitable scandal, and Cicely lost favour with the press in which it was concluded that her disappearance had been nothing more than an elaborate publicity stunt.

As interest in the story abated life at Oakfield soon

resumed its usual pattern, and by spring of the following year Cicely had completed the first draft of what is perhaps her most complex work – *Murder in the Maze* (1929). The novel is set in the auspicious surroundings of Hampton Court and elevates the character of Crichton Gable from the status of 'a proletarian gumshoe' (*Crimes Monthly*, Mar. 1927), as one anonymous critic unkindly calls him, to that of such eminent detectives as G.S. Trevelyan's Inspector Mull, or perhaps even Sir Edward Preston's inimitable Hogarth Slater. However, and typical of Cicely's sense of irony, Gable is initially mistaken for an impertinent gardener by the party of distressed debutantes whom he eventually leads from peril. *Murder in the Maze* also marks the arrival of the loveable but highly accident prone Dr Tippet, a creation familiar to the genre who follows the hero everywhere and is devised to solicit questions that the perceptive reader might want to ask.

In the summer of 1938, Cicely made a whistle-stop tour of the eastern states of America, where she became the toast of New York's literary elite and was showered with honours by the people of Chelsea, a location that features so prominently in *Two Left Feet* (1936). The book was adapted for the American market from the short story called 'Golden Graham', which appears in a collection entitled *Bloody Justice* (1935). The story finds Gable holidaying in Massachusetts where he is reluctantly persuaded by the city's mayor to locate the football team's promising young quarterback, following his abduction by an overlooked college rival.

In Boston Cicely was invited to speak before a select audience at Harvard University, where she delivered an eloquent lecture on the 'locked-room' scenario, a puzzle-oriented mystery that at first seems baffling but is later discovered to have a perfectly rational explanation. In 'Chambers & Co.', for instance, another jewel from *Bloody Justice*, Mr Grubb is found asphyxiated in the company's strong-room, the door to which can only be locked from the outside. Given the genuine repugnance of the young accountant's character murder is immediately assumed, but Gable's examination of the scene reveals that the door has the ability to close of its own accord and, 'if allowed to do so from its maximum extent, would slam with enough force to throw the bolts'.

Cicely returned to England in autumn 1938, yet, at the height of her powers and by now a wealthy woman, no further book appeared for over a decade, during which time and removed from the public gaze, she dutifully assisted her second husband the Rev. Stevens in his profession and parish life.

Following the reverend's death in November 1948, Cicely broke from the confines of Oakfield and took a house on the island of Malta where, in under a year and to the delight of her expectant readers, she produced three titles that are imbued with intrigue and Mediterranean flavour.

Cicely was made President of the British Crime Writers' Guild in 1959 and, in the same year, she won the esteemed Sir Edward Preston Memorial Trophy, an award that many felt was long overdue. In the Queen's birthday honours list of 1960, Cicely received the MBE, yet she was always denied membership of the prestigious London Society of Sleuths, which even today remains an exclusively male preserve.

Cicely Carrington's books have sold in their millions and are translated into over 40 languages. Many have been adapted for the cinema and television, while the long running stage play of *Dinner is Served* (1929) still continues to delight audiences in London's West End.

Strange then, it seems, that in April 1971, following the triumph of what became her last book, *O'Casey's Comeuppance* (1970), the author was intending to dispense with Crichton Gable and retire this timeless figure from public life. A contributing factor may have been that, although Cicely continued to produce on average one novel a year, the necessity for new and ever more fantastic Gable adventures on television required the employment of several ghost writers to meet the demand.

In June 1968, Cicely had signed a loosely worded contract with executives of a US television production company and subsequently lost control of her creation. The result finds Gable in all manner of implausible situations, from settling land disputes with native Americans to restoring order to the nation's capital following the defeat of aliens from outer space.

Although there is nothing to suggest that this dispute, which Cicely was unable to resolve through numerous lawyers and at great expense, was in any way connected with the events of April 6, Cicely's accident could be seen to resemble the scenario from *Portrait of a Murderer* (1951), in which a successful young artist is mown down by the speeding Bentley of his agent. The painter has expressed the wish to depart from his usual landscapes and concentrate on less popular experimental compositions, while the disreputable gallery owner destroys his client to push up the price of his work and dispose of additional fakes that he has commissioned from abroad.

On the day in question Cicely had arranged to lunch with her publicist Gloria Fitzsimmons at 1.30pm in dinning room of the Grand Hotel, but she instructed her driver to drop her at the top of Union Street at 12pm – over a mile from this location.

Shortly after, with the chauffeur out of sight and 'hastening across the road towards some unknown destination, she was thrown off her feet by the motorcycle' (*Torbay Evening Enquirer*, Apr. 7, 1971).

Curiously, neither the chauffeur Gerald Spears, who committed suicide a week later, nor Miss Fitzsimmons, who was killed in a car crash that summer, reported Cicely's disappearance. Both, however, were at her bedside in a private room of the hospital – along with three business associates and a lawyer from her publishing company – when she passed away in the early hours of the following morning.

The motorcycle and its rider have never been traced.

Speculation as to why Cicely was early and so far from her appointment is uncertain, yet one theory is that she had arranged a meeting with members of the then prominent Women's Liberation Movement, to which she is thought to have often lent support.

Sarah Kirkpatrick, a leading figure of the group, maintained that the meeting had been agreed by telephone, and although she later informed police of the arrangement the matter was never investigated.

On the day before she was due to give evidence at the Coroner's inquest, where it was deemed Cicely had died of heart failure, 'Miss Kirkpatrick was found drowned in the bath when her landlord had been forced to break down the washroom door' (*Torquay Gazette*, Apr. 9, 1971).

In July 1996, Martin Brady was compelled to resign early from a life-time's work with the NHS when, following a tip-off from his astute neighbour, police raided the nurse's home and found 'a substantial quantity of confidential medical records and assorted papers' (*Nursing Monthly News*, Aug. 1996). The material was returned to his employer and Brady was given a six month suspended sentence, but among the collection were some faded papers of unknown origin that eventually found their way to the salerooms of a disreputable firm of London auctioneers.

As well as their weekly sale of furniture, household goods and electric appliances, Webster's of Soho once cornered the lucrative market in disposing of miscellaneous documents that often surface after the death of an aspiring writer. These items, with a little tailoring and in the right market, can often return a modest profit and include all manner of written material, such as personal and professional correspondence, diaries, ledgers, research notes and autobiographical recollections. In addition, there are rejected poems, short stories, children's fairy tales, the outlines of uncommissioned television and radio dramas, impractical theatre plays, loquacious film scripts, but most prolific of all is the unfinished novel.

Although at first dismissed as an obvious forgery, the pages were bought by an anonymous enthusiast and were later verified as the undoubted work of Cicely Carrington. Today they are under glass at Oakfield which, having lain empty for several years and allowed to fall into disrepair, is now a museum, made possible with funds from the National Lottery. From their tone it is obvious that Cicely was intending to draw a discreet veil over the detective's life, possibly to concentrate on other projects or perhaps even retire herself.

The intended work, ominously entitled *Gable's End*, seems also to express great consideration for Cicely's readers by carefully forewarning them of eventual outcome. Equally, the opening passage, which is reproduced below, demonstrates a change of pace towards the subdued and reflective, and although Crichton Gabel appears to be heading for an albeit reluctant new beginning, regrettably it is the last thing that 'C.C.' ever wrote.

Chapter One

December. Sunday. Twilight.

Gable sat alone at his usual table in Mrs Whittle's Tea Shop and calmly poured the remainder of the pot into the cup before him. With his elbows leaning casually on the table, he palmed the cup in both hands and gazed vacantly through the window at the street beyond – empty save for the odd soul on his way to church or an evening train.

The chairs were rising about him as Old Sam's mop swept like a ballerina across the monochrome tiled floor, leaving a dull patch and the debris of afternoon tea at the detective's feet.

Behind the cleared marble counter, as the great urn cooled to silence, an ancient wireless was relaying the service from a nearby cathedral.

Gable, indifferent to the hymns and canticles, remained immobile, engrossed in his thoughts and only vaguely aware of the sudden announcement that had interrupted the ceremony – something to do with the number five.

'Fifth. The fifth, perhaps?' thought Gable. 'The fifth what?'

Old Sam's brows veered at the news and he strained with the dials for reception, but Gable showed less than a passing interest, preferring instead to indulge himself with the idle observation of an injured pidgin pulling at scraps in the gutter outside.

'Fifth,' the voice called to him in his mind

again, which irritated and distracted Gable from his leisurely pursuit. Gradually, however, and by increasing degrees awareness was restored, and his senses finally tuned completely to hear the cup smash on its saucer and the voice scream at him like the headline of a morning newspaper: '5th BODY FOUND IN THAMES'.

For a second he could not move, incredulous to the thought that he had allowed himself a moment's repose and to fall into such a frivolous stupor.

He turned to Old Sam for assurance, but the cleaner simply replied with a discerning glance and turned away to extinguish his cigarette in the sink.

Gable leapt to his feet and flew at the door tearing his coat from the stand, which spun on its base and toppled breaking one of the hooks. In alarm he reached in his pockets and pulled out a handful of coins, which he pressed upon the old man before tripping on the step and falling out into the street.

Without a thought for his badly grazed hands, Gable's eyes darted to and fro for a taxi, but with the streets deserted, and after a third impatient examination of his naked wrist, he ran to the nearby tube station and proceeded towards the Tottenham Court Road, where he would have to change before heading north to his Camden Town residence on the High Street.

How stupid he was to find himself

daydreaming on the wrong side of London and a meeting with Inspector Driscoll set for less than half an hour's time, while the documents pertaining to the case, given to him for his perusal three days before, still lay unopened on the window seat of his study.

Arriving home Gable did not even wait for Mrs Arnold to answer the front door, but instead he let himself into the hall and shot past the mountain of packing cases and up the stairs.

He paused by the door to his study and sighed remorsefully as he recalled the last time when he had entered that room. On the previous morning he had specifically instructed the removers to refrain from any activity in his personal sanctum until the following Monday – when he would be present to supervise the work for himself. Mrs Arnold, however, whom he had failed to similarly inform, had directed them otherwise, and Gable had returned in the evening to find many things disturbed and was uncharacteristically brusque and short with the men.

Typically (and fortunately for Gable) the policeman was late, and the detective hurried expectantly into his study in the hope of enjoying a quiet moment to collect himself and contemplate the relevant material with which he had been entrusted.

He fell exhausted into the soft armchair as the embers of a coal fire, lit for an earlier hour, dwindled at his feet.

The solemn granite-cased chronometer, an indebted token of esteem from His Holiness Pope Pius XII for the safe recovery of the holy relic St Benedict's Toe, was still ticking on the mantleshelf – even though, at Gable's insistence, it had not been wound in over a week, should any movement of the clock while the main spring was coiled prove harmful to the mechanism. There too was the famous Hartlepool Dagger, an appreciative offering from its previous owner, the distinguished Viscount Tooley, whose daughter had been stabbed with the article, and Gable had pinpointed her reluctant fiancé as the perpetrator. Beside it, but no less prominent in its ivory and iron wood mount, was the jealously guarded de Witt Gem, a flawless stone from the Cape, gifted with all generosity from the mine owner Johannes de Witt following Gable's shrewd exposition of ubiquitous diamond pilfering among his workforce.

Below Gable's eyes rested on the wicker chair from dear Jessie MacMaster's cottage in the Scotch Highlands, where Gable on a coastal walk had sought refuge from the haar and inadvertently stumbled upon a gang of bloodthirsty cut-throats who were in league with high-ranking officials of the Third Reich.

Clearly visible on the left front leg was the bullet that had shattered poor Gable's knee and imbedded itself in the wood, while on the arms were abrasions from the coarse bindings that had restrained him before he had managed to free himself and summon help on the enemy's discarded radio set in the adjacent barn.

Draped around the chair's back was Gable's trademark harlequin waistcoat, embroidered with colourful parallelograms and pendulous with the gold hunter and chain that had been triumphantly won in a test of wits with the shameless prankster Shamus O'Casey, even though the watch had never ticked a second in its life.

Gable allowed himself a modest smile at the victory, but his heart soon sank as his eyes fell again upon the glossy brochures illustrating the Sunnyvale Retirement Flats which, to his annoyance, had been requested from Slough and now adorned the chair's seat.

He would certainly miss the old room in which he had spent so many satisfying hours in thought and entertained several eminent figures of European society. The statesmen of the age once beat a relentless path to his door, each with a seemingly mystifying conundrum for him to contemplate and decipher, yet that path was less trodden these days except, of course, by the hapless Inspector Driscoll of Scotland Yard, who was always in need of assistance.

Gable looked despondently around his study and strained through the moisture in his eyes that now distorted the familiar forms of his prized possessions. Every item about him rekindled some moment of his life that might otherwise be lost to the passage of time. Unfortunately, however, he would have to leave behind many of the treasured things with which he had surrounded himself over the years. The great walrus tusk, for instance, intricately chiselled and hanging above the door – a parting gift from the appreciative Captain Jake Larsen of the whaling ship *Ventura* for Gable's efforts in identifying Shem Proops as the murderer of Tippet the cabin boy (who had tragically rejected the first mate's advances) – would not be accompanying him to his new home. Likewise, the polished elephant's foot, a hollowed and invaluable receptacle for Gable's many canes and umbrellas that was sawn from the beast Lord Hayward bagged on safari in Kenya – shortly before the game warden's assistant Inky fell foul of His Lordship's wrath – must also remain where it stood.

In the window, still unfinished, was the matchstick model of Chancery Lane, Temple and Lincoln's Inn Fields over which Gable had laboured tirelessly for the last three decades and intended to bestow upon Judge Strickland's widow Juliana, who had so captivated him on their first meeting. How much simpler it would have been, mused Gable regrettably, if only he had told her his feelings at the time.

In the street below Gable could hear the

customary Sunday evening sounds of horses' hooves and market traders pulling their carts over the cobbled stones and making their way home after a long but satisfying day.

Gable's eyes closed and he sank back into the chair where soon he fell to sleep – as the mantle clock gave out its last and the pendulum swung diminishingly towards its final resting place.

Equator

(zero degrees latitude)

Northern waste along the clock
Revolves; and on, as though ill-timed, will
    GULP; BUT PULL UP TUB PLUG
South equator, water flows
Reversed in line.

NB On the scale of a household bath the Coriolis Effect, as this phenomenon is called, has never been successfully proved.

Offside

Some people, perhaps new to the game, can find the rules of association football confusing – to say the least. Although they are of no great consequence, this minority of usually transient and often indifferent spectators, who are uncertain of the sport's relatively simple regulations, will frequently ruin the enjoyment of any match for the vast majority with a barrage of incessant but elementary questions. These enquiries can range anywhere from repeated demands for the definition of technical terms, like 'goal difference', through more searching investigations of the penalty shoot-out, to the ultimate 'How long does this go on for?' the answer to which seems destined never to register. However, there is no rule that creates more ambiguity within the ranks of the incognisant than the *position* of 'offside'. Much has been written on the subject, and many hours spent in extensive but fruitless explanation – sadly resulting in nothing more than domestic estrangement. Yet adequate comprehension of the offside *position* is entirely possible by anyone in whom there exists the slightest glimmer of intelligence.

Equally important is the ability to recognise an offside *offence* when it occurs – another common misunderstanding. The seemingly unjustified decision, compounded by the award of an indirect free kick, will frequently generate a wave of hostility towards match officials, who must then endure the inevitable but gratuitous flood of ill-informed verbal abuse. Such occasions, fuelled by ignorance, only serve to augment superfluous friction within the otherwise healthy rivalry that exists between opposing supporters and may also lead to unsightly exhibitions of pernicious behaviour and even physical violence.

In an effort to arrest the obvious disquiet that surrounds this most elusive of sporting maxims, the 'Offside Rule', as defined in the latest edition of the highly respected *Bentwhistle's Rules of Soccer* (SFA Press, 2004), is reproduced below with additional notes for the uninitiated.

Rule 11 – Offside

A player is in an offside position when he (or she remember, because women play football these days too, you know – bless them) *is nearer to his opponent's goal line than both the ball and the second last player of the opposing team, except when he is in his own half of the pitch.* (That's the sort of square grassy thing with the white lines painted on it.)

This in itself is not an offence, as any linesman will tell you. However, *a player in the offside position may be penalised when the ball is played by a member of the same team* (at any hour of the day, on any day of the week, come rain or shine, hell or high water and even during the dying seconds of extra time; regardless of score, league position or championship status) *if the referee* (who, believe it or not, is also human, subject to close scrutiny by the governing body of his profession and certainly not immune from accusations of favouritism; irrespective of sex, colour, race, nationality, religion, political affiliation, perceived ability, intellect, physical or mental deficiency, sexual preference/deviance and/or questionable parentage; notwithstanding metaphoric allegiance with bodily emissions, the posterior or male/female genitalia, whether or not engaged in acts of masturbation or sexual intercourse) *considers that player to be involved in active play.*

‘Wodewick Th-Th-Th... twoud’

> And I saw a new heaven and a new earth: for the first heaven and the first earth were passed away; and there was no more sea. *Revelation* 21:1

On the afternoon of July 20, 1969, the respected British news agency Ariel Inc. announced ‘an outbreak of mass-hysteria at Hyde Park in London’. Over 50 people were affected, ‘consumed’, it is said, ‘by infectious laughter’ and many had been led from the scene ‘reduced to tears, while others required medical treatment to ease their condition’. The exact cause was never confirmed, and news of the incident was later eclipsed by events unfolding some 384,403 km away – as Apollo 11 prepared to land on the surface of the moon. Intriguingly, however, in an interview with *Pond Lining Monthly* (Apr. 1980), Harry H. Fowler OBE, while reminiscing on ‘40 glorious years as boatman in the Royal Park’ and wholeheartedly endorsing the unrivalled attributes of ‘Le Marche Noir 1500 (deluxe)’, recalls when he had occasion to extricate Pastor Jo Mancini from the Serpentine on the eve of his retirement precisely one week before.

Pastor Jo, as he was affectionately known, had become involved in a heated theological debate at Speakers’ Corner with Roderick Stroud, ‘one of that anti-nuclear mob’, says Fowler, in which the pastor had gained the upper hand and Stroud had lost two of his front teeth. Stroud was removed from the park after questioning by police, but the pastor, who had bolted across the grass, unwittingly ran headlong into the water to be rescued by Fowler. He was taken by ambulance to Westminster Hospital, but discharged himself that evening and returned alone to his Paddington lodgings where, in the early hours of the following morning, he 'suffocated on vomit caused by an excessive intake of alcohol' (Dr A. Manners, *J.D.L. Mancini, Death Certificate*, Jul. 14, 1969).

Joseppie Donarto Luigi Mancini was a familiar figure in the park and a regular speaker on Sunday afternoons. He originally came from the quiet fishing village of Spugna, which is consistently the wettest place in Italy. As a boy he spent Christmas with relatives in Massina, until 1908 when an earthquake severely damaged the town and a tidal wave swept away the home of his great-uncle Domenico and his entire family.

In the 1920s, Mancini lived in Venice where he worked as a gondolier, but he was forced to leave the city when his dilapidated lodgings collapsed into the Grand Canal, killing his fiancée and 12 others (trans. *Arresto News*, Mar. 6, 1928). He arrived in Britain in the winter of 1942 with the remains of a defeated military unit that was captured by the 8th Army in the Western Desert during the North African campaign. Following months in detention and an arduous journey to Liverpool, he was sent north and held at Camp 60 on the island of Lamb Holm in Orkney, where he worked on the Churchill Barriers around Scapa Flow, connecting the islands with the mainland and forming a safe anchorage for the British Home Fleet.

The desolation and harsh conditions of Lamb Holm could not have been further from his Mediterranean origins. However, after the Italian capitulation in September 1943, greater freedom was given to prisoners and a few weeks later '324 Mancini, J.D.L., Sgt, XXI Corps, 2nd Libyan Div., escaped from the island in a stolen drifter, much to the surprise of Corporal G. Sinclair and assistant postmistress Miss Katrina Munro, neither of whom saw him flee the Kirkwall Post Office at some time between 11.30am and 12.15pm' (Col. S. Huxley, *Commandant's Report*, Oct. 15, 1943). The boat was discovered three days later floating in the shallow waters of Dunnet Bay on the north coast of Scotland, 'overturned and defiantly unseaworthy having possibly been in collision with another vessel' (PC J. McEwan, *Notebook*, Oct.-Dec. 1943). Meanwhile, Mancini had gone to ground and survived undetected in the hills of Caithness and Sutherland for the remainder of the war.

He surfaced again when he was arrested for 'gross exuberance' (*West Highland Echo*, Nov. 7, 1945) on the streets of Oban during the town's unofficial Bonfire Night celebrations. Mancini, however, managed to evade repatriation and, through the intervention of the Rev. Helmut Drood from the nearby Free Presbyterian Church, a ministry offering moralising and sombre worship that verges on the puritan, he was naturalised as a British citizen the following year.

What relationship there was between Mancini, a staunch Catholic in his youth, and the Rev. Drood remains speculation, but he must have turned to him during his years in the wilderness, while his isolation as a fugitive could account for his 'many eccentricities' as Fowler calls them.

However, it would be more than 20 years before Mancini began his Hyde Park sermons and for part of that time he lived in Glasgow, where he ran a small shoe repair business that specialised in the recovery of waterproof boots – a skill that he had learnt in Italy and perfected on Lamb Holm.

In September 1953, he married Nellie McMurdo, the daughter of Wilson McMurdo, butcher and sole supplier of the very successful west-coast delicacy McMurdo's Stodge, an advanced form of boiled dumpling that not surprisingly 'niver fails tae fill ye up', as the accompanying slogan once ran. The marriage, however, ended sadly two years later when 'Nellie Mancini was dragged unconscious from the bottom of the Gallowgate municipal swimming baths and pronounced dead on arrival at the city's Royal Infirmary' (*Glasgow Tribune*, Aug. 8, 1955). The tragedy obviously devastated Mancini and seems also to have affected the balance of his mind. He immediately abandoned his home and business and set off on a 10-year pilgrimage of North and Central America, during which time he formulated a self-styled religion that would later 'captivate an audience with his unique blend of expressive theatre and religious zeal, while prophesying imminent divine retribution and impending apocalyptic doom' (Reggie Mossett, 'On a Stroll Through the Park', *The Bohemian*, Mar. 1967).

Mancini was also prone to frequent outbursts and fits of violence due, suggests Fowler, 'to his Latin temperament', although it was widely rumoured that in favourable conditions he could receive certain high-frequency off-shore radio broadcasts via a steel plate that was inserted in his head after a diving accident in Acapulco, where, in a boast with locals and the worst for drink, he had mistimed a wave. Fowler concludes that 'Pastor Jo was something of loose cannon – liable to fire at any time, which was probably why he was so popular.'

Roderick Stroud, on the other hand, was a devout atheist and something of a novice when it came to public speaking. Fowler vaguely recalls 'some toffee-nosed bearded character with a hearing-aid, who was in serious need of a bath'.

Stroud was born on VE Day, 1945, in the small hamlet of Wading in England, south-west of The Wash on reclaimed land of the Lincolnshire Marsh. His father worked at a nearby market garden and the family, his elder sister and mother, occupied the house that was once owned by Lord Dregs, who immortalised the village in his famous poem 'The Wading Wait' (1847).

Wading high and Wading low,
The rain doth rain and the wind doth blow,
Longing for a love to show,
Coming from the marsh.

The family holidayed at Skegness or Mablethorpe during the summer, although, on a spring vacation to Cromer, Roderick and his father went missing for several hours in a small rowing boat and were eventually 'washed ashore dishevelled but otherwise unscathed at Great Yarmouth, much to the delight of a group of day-trippers from Felixstowe' (*Norwich Herald*, Apr. 15, 1949).

At the age of six Stroud appeared in an amateur production of *Noah's Ark* in which he played the back end of the Unicorn, a performance described by one critic as 'thoroughly convincing and not at all bad for a first attempt' (Pricilla Glamtoby-Smyth, *The Wading Gargle*, Jun. 16, 1951).

When he was seven his parents were separated and Roderick and his sister moved with their mother to her home town of Lynmouth in Devon. The town derives its name from an old Anglo-Saxon term meaning 'the town on the torrent' and was annihilated by a flash flood on August 15, 1952.

The children returned to Wading where Roderick soon abandoned his schooling, preferring instead to be educated at home and accompany his father on frequent business trips to the Netherlands. On February 1, 1953, they were staying at a small guesthouse in the village of Kortgene in Zeeland. Shortly before dawn 50 of Holland's primary sea defences crumbled into the North Sea and within minutes more than 100 towns and villages were under water. Roderick spent the following week at the home of family friends in Rotterdam when, unbelievably, news arrived of gale-force winds and accompanying high tides that caused severe flooding across Lincolnshire and washed away the entire village of Wading with great loss of life (trans. *Ochtendblad*, Feb. 4, 1953).

Stroud remained at the Vanderberg residence until September 1956, when he was enrolled in the famous Victor Streeble Institute near Haarlem, 'a pioneering establishment that stresses the importance of maintaining human equilibrium with nature' (*VSI Prospectus*, Eng. ed., 2004). The school moved to purpose-built premises on the outskirts of Haarlem in 1964, but the original building still survives and is precariously situated on the polder below the famous dike that the little Dutch boy stuck his finger in to stem a leak and save the town. Stroud, however, lasted only one term at the VSI before he left without any explanation, although it is said that he had frequently expressed a desire to travel (trans. Prof. J. Oort, *Letter to Mr R. Vanderberg*, Dec. 13, 1956).

Interestingly, the famous science fiction writer O.G. Blotch attended the same school and was a contemporary of Stroud's. In the third book of the very successful 'Nordock' series entitled *Glug, Glug, Glug* (1971), the central character is a young Hajan with the curious name Twoud. Twoud is ridiculed by the inhabitants of Phocan, a major trading post in the province of Haja on the planet Uh, for suggesting that the nearby 'slogmatt', a type of volcano that has lain dormant for nearly 300 'quargarts', could erupt at any 'quam'. Twoud is proved right, and the townsfolk are left squabbling over the remaining 'flams' and 'flamwangs' (vehicles and escape pods) as an encroaching sea of acid engulfs the town. Meanwhile, Twoud and his family watch from the safety of their 'flimflamwang' before setting off to begin their new life on Ta – over 70 'kloghorts' away.

In Chapter Two of the novel, Twoud is playing innocently at the base of the 'slogmatt' when he discovers the volatile condition of the volcano and tries to warn his fellow Hajans:

> 'Vimcan, vorcan, veecan, va,' sang Twoud merrily as he rounded a large dromadom and plucked the ripest lumlum from its brotch.
>
> 'Qwaga!' he exclaimed to himself and wiped the sticky eegue from the three corners of his smiling plooth with the end of his tattered hofflechop.
>
> The pom shone warmly across the vast Haja plains, even though it was almost mid-gwimble, and Twoud lay down in the shade of a large jomflot and quickly fell into a deep mooze.
>
> After about thirty quams he awoke and found that the ground beneath him was shaking violently. Twoud was pomtrifust, and he leapt to his flomps but could not hold his balance and fell to thc ground again, where he crawled about through the rising dust in sheer terribot.
>
> 'Hoowif, hoowif!' he cried in vain, as there was no one around for klogs, but after a few quams the ground settled and everything was quiet again.

Twoud stood up and looked about. There was a great crevasse at his flomps that ran all the way up the side of the slogmatt. The ground had ruptured and just below the surface was a fast-flowing river of blue wedda that gave off a foul smeg. The river was obviously twixoc, and Twoud could see that Phocan was directly in its path. He would have to hurry and warn the Hajans of Phocan, but before Twoud could do anything the ground began shaking again and once more he was thrown off his flomps.

Twoud thought that the whole of Uh was about to swashel him up, but the tremor soon stopped and when the dust had settled for a second time there was no crevasse or poisonous river anywhere. The ground had closed up and hidden it, but Twoud knew that the river was still beneath him and heading straight for Phocan.

Twoud picked up his bibblegob and his two splogpats, but forgot all about his gobblefop (something that no self-respecting Hajan would ever be seen without), and he ran as fast as his little gogs could carry him all the way to Phocan.

When he got the centre of Phocan he found that a large crowd had gathered there to welcome the newly elected Mofflehop, who was parading through Phocan on an enormous hom. Twoud climbed to the top of the highest troob and called out: ‘Hajans vee Phocan. Brogwot ra slogmatt! Brogwot ra slogmatt!’ But the other Hajans just ignored him, preferring instead to watch the new

Mofflehop riding high on his purpose built hom.

Twoud got down from the troob and desperately pushed his way through the crowd until he was right in front of the approaching Mofflehop. He furiously waved his amdibs and called out for the Mofflehop to stop and listen to what he had to say.

'Brogwot ra slogmatt,' he called again but could not be heard above the noise of the excited Hajans.

When the hom was almost upon him the new Mofflehop suddenly gave the signal to stop and for everyone to be quiet. He then dismounted and slomped towards Twoud, who was by now completely poopledrooped. The Mofflehop placed a kindly droog on Twoud's shem and softly asked him to repeat what he had said.

'Brogwot ra slogmatt,' replied Twoud timidly after a moment's hesitation, and everyone gasped in fear and disbelief.

The new Mofflehop looked very carefully at Twoud, thought for a qwam, then turned and calmly announced to the Hajans of Phocan: 'Fesswig ra slogmatt vin rensum ta gobblefop.' Suddenly everyone burst into loud smiggles, while the new Mofflehop pointed an accusing digwot at Twoud.

'Plem lo gobblefop?' asked the new Mofflehop, and everyone began to chant:

'Plem lo gobblefop? Plem lo gobblefop?'

Twoud looked down and saw that he was

> indeed without his trusty gobblefop, and he slomped off ashamedly with the crowd's smiggles ranging in his twegs.

In early 1962, Roderick Stroud was living in a basement apartment that was leased by a young English woman in Wedel on the outskirts of Hamburg. Janet Bennington had moved to Germany with her father Colonel Basil 'Bulwark' Bennington, who was stationed at Celle and was nearing the end of distinguished career with the Royal Engineers. On the evening of August 5, 1961, 'following an otherwise uneventful cocktail party in the officer's mess' (*Forces Weekly News*, Aug 10, 1961), Janet absconded from the base and vanished for several months without trace. The colonel's ceaseless attempts to discover his daughter's whereabouts were in vain, and he returned to England in December 1961, where he retired to the seclusion of his Sussex home.

On February 17, 1962, waters of the North Sea, stirred by a violent storm, swept over Germany's seawalls and roared inland. Rivers and streams were swollen to bursting, and the Elbe River in particular rose to an unprecedented height. Krautsand, Bremen and Hamburg were engulfed by the speed of the assault, and other towns and affected outlying areas of rich agricultural land took months to recover. Around 500,000 people were made homeless and over 300 drowned.

Colonel B. Bennington was eventually reunited with his daughter 'at St Peter's Church, on March 2,

1962, 3pm', while 'close friends and relatives only' were invited to present themselves 'thereafter at The Manse, Sidley, East Sussex. Flowers to Mr H. Ghoul & Sons, Hastings' (*Times Newspaper*, Feb. 28, 1962).

Roderick Stroud spent much of the same day in a police cell near Heathrow Airport, 'for entering the country with insufficient documents, and was questioned by officers of the Special Branch over matters relating to national security' (*West London Post*, Mar. 3, 1962). Stroud was held for 48 hours but released from custody without charge.

In the summer of 1967, under the pseudonym Rodger Stirling, Prof. H.J. Glottal of the visionary South London College of Meteorology and Applied Linguistics submitted a short story to a writing competition, which enticed contestants with 'the grand prize of £25 for the winner and other substantial rewards for successful runners-up' (*Metropolitan Monthly Sketch*, Jun. 1967). Unfortunately the professor failed to secure a return for his efforts, but a shortened version of the story appeared in the Christmas edition of the magazine along with five others, all of which 'exhibited considerable promise' and were collectively entitled 'The Best of the Rest'.

The story concerns itself with a middle-aged and reserved, somewhat set-in-his-ways, university professor who suddenly discovers the possibility of London being flooded in the event of extreme high tides and the urgent need for substantial downstream barriers to protect the capital. After years of dogged persistence, during which time he is ostracised by his peers and subjected to scorn and derision from London authorities, the professor's dream is eventually realised and, exactly one week from 'a delightful opening ceremony in which HRH Princess Anne names the barrier The Glottal Stop', the device is tested to its limit and withstands the very tide that the professor had predicted. The story has few merits, other than its foresight, yet the moment of realisation – when the professor envisages London extinguished – is possibly the most noteworthy.

> I was standing alone on Waterloo Bridge, as I often do, and gazed downstream in the fading light of a summer evening, while profusions of cumulonimbus clouds were swept majestically across an otherwise clear blue sky by the prevailing north-easterly breeze.
>
> I glanced idly at the banks, both left and right, and then watched downstream in horror as, in the distance and driving towards me at a height and rate of knots that I could scarcely believe, there came inland from the sea a great wave.
>
> The water soared high above the buildings, toppling and splintering them into matchwood. Boats and ships were ripped from their moorings or blown into vapour, and bridge after bridge was severed from its piles and cast aside like the pulling of a troublesome root.
>
> The city, the spot where I stood and everything suddenly vanished, and I saw a huge ocean from above, detached from the scene and

removed, with no sign of land nor anything that had been before.

I felt both sheer elation and blind terror in one and the same moment, but I soon returned unscathed to familiar surroundings for nothing untoward had occurred. 'Swoosh', *MMS* (Dec. 1967)

Roderick Stroud attended the SLSMAL from 1964 to 1967, where he studied air quality, climate variation and diction. As well as the final examination, a further requirement for completion of the course was the submission of a paper of 'not more than 4000 words that demonstrates qualitative research and original thought' (*SLSMAL Course Handbook*, 1964). Stroud received the mark 'C+' from Prof. Glottal for an essay entitled 'London in Peril' in May 1967, and although all other essays for that year are accounted for in the school's library, Stroud's is missing.

The Thames Barrier was raised for the first time on October 1, 1982. There is no suggestion that the professor's story played any part in its conception.

During his studies, however, Stroud became involved with a radical and early form of environmental pressure group known as SWIM (Social Wealth in Moderation), which called for 'a reduction in the rate of capitalist growth and free swimming lessons for all' (*SWIM Manifesto*, 1965-6). Stroud abandoned the group on the first anniversary of its founding, following a weekend trip to Blackpool when an unofficial motion was passed advocating 'Indirect Violent Action, Unconditional Sex and Free Beer'

(*Adulterated 'Kiss-Me-Quick' Hat*, *c.* 1966).

Apart from this youthful diversion into organised politics, Stroud was never a member of any political party or environmental movement, perhaps due to the often diverse interests of such groups. Instead, he preferred to campaign alone and against what he saw was the single principal issue – global pollution.

As well as demonstrating in London, Roderick Stroud visited Sweden in 1972, where he was seen parading with a placard, written in Swedish advising To Hills the Take, which proved an amusing diversion for arriving delegates of the Stockholm Conference.

In 1982, Stroud was in Kenya where he was held in police custody for the duration of the United Nations Environment Conference, following 'a reckless prank that involved the distribution of over 100 pairs of galoshes, thrown from a speeding van, outside the headquarters of the UN Environment Program' (*Nairobi Daily News*, May 11, 1982). Stroud was also present at the famous Earth Summit in Rio de Janeiro in 1992, where he was due to speak at a fringe meeting held by a disparate group calling themselves The Pals of the Planet, but he cancelled at the last minute after an argument over the seating arrangements.

In 1997, Roderick Stroud was in Kyoto in Japan where, with the assistance of the noted elocution master Prof. A.H. Phlegm, he successfully lobbied the Clinton administration negotiators to agree to legally binding international enforceable limits on the emission of greenhouse gasses.

However, when crusading in the late-1960s, Roderick Stroud not only had to compete with anti-war protestors, supporters of the women's movement, race activists and left-wing radicals, his message was possibly hindered by a pronounced southern English accent with r-less pronunciation, a severe lisp and crippling stammer.

On Sunday afternoons in Hyde Park, while desperately trying to awaken people to what he believed were the dangers that threatened their very existence, Stroud would often refer to a concise pamphlet that outlines his concerns. Stroud's anxiety for the future may be seen to border on acute paranoia, but his observations could anticipate the possible detriment to the planet from such phenomena as global warming, acid rain and the effects of deforestation.

CATASTROPHIC CRISIS PREDICTED

Trouble Brewing for Future Generations

Solar Structure Ruined Irreparably

Rapid and remorseless increase of world industrialisation could result in soaring temperatures as warmth from the sun's rays becomes trapped and accentuated by the polluted atmosphere.

Sudden Sea-Surge Certain

Polar regions may reduce in size as levels of snow and ice diminish, while several specific areas, including much of Great Britain, could disappear under rapidly rising seas.

> *Tornados, Cyclones and Hurricanes*
> Extreme weather could prevail and severe storms, once strangers to our shores, may become a common occurrence.
> *Rainfall in this Region*
> Corrosive rain could precipitate prolifically and cause small streams and rivers to swell into raging torrents, accentuating the threat of drowning.
> *Creatures at Risk*
> Widespread destruction of tropical forests will certainly prove harmful to a rich array of natural species, such as rodents, rare birds and reptiles.
> R.S. Esq. (*c.* Jun. 1969)

President George W. Bush withdrew America from the Kyoto Protocol in March 2001. In the same month Roderick Stroud was seen heading towards Kathmandu in Nepal, south of the Himalayan Ridge – approximately 1220 metres above sea level.

Just Junk

Personal Assurance, Home Insurance,
Securing Loans since 1908;
Congratulations! Great Inventions,
How to meet Your Perfect Mate!

Frozen Food at Frozen Prices,
Special Offers (pound for pound),
Meals Galore – the family store,
Massive savings all year round;

Double Glazing, Fitted Kitchens,
Bathroom Suites – full range of tiles;
Home Extensions, Crime Prevention,
Driveways Surfaced – every style;

Cars! Cars! Cars! Cars!
Motorbikes, Small Trucks and Vans,
Buying, Trading (cond. depending),
Honest Prices (cash in hand);

Mobiles, TVs, CDs, PCs,
DVDs – all interest free;
Easy Payment: 12 instalments
(direct debit guarantee);

Subscribe Today, Send No Money,
Order quickly while stocks last
(finely crafted moulded plastic)
MADE IN CHINA, Selling Fast!

Maharajahs, Children Welcome
(4 till 6, no under fives),
Classic Menu, Bring Your Own Brew!
(Minimal corkage charge applies);

Tell Your Friends and Get Connected,
Lowest Rates you'll ever pay!*
Netherlands 2p per minute
**Internet £10 a day...*

Bill's Will

Remember me a little then, I pray,
The idle singer of an empty day.
William Morris
'An Apology', *The Earthly Paradise* (1868)

Penbury Manor was a large but unpretentious building that stood for over a century on raised ground above approximately 2000 acres of rolling Wiltshire countryside. The house was built in the late-18th century by Sir Thomas Stokes, a local merchant and successful businessman who amassed a considerable fortune in the county's profitable cloth trade.

Stokes Hall, as it was then called, remained with the family until 1795 when Sir Thomas Stokes, an elderly widower and father of eight daughters, was stripped of the house, its contents and 'some of the finest farmland in England', in a wager with Hubert Penbury during 'a congenial weekend of festive music, company and amusement' (Miss Elisa Stokes, *Invitation to Mr Guy Osborne & Friends*, Dec. 22, 1794).

Beyond the gatehouse, a somewhat ostentatious 19th-century addition, the main approach crosses the A345 at Fritteringale and veers down a steep gradient to where it levels beside an isolated tributary of the river Avon. Over the small stone bridge to the left there is a quaint row of terraced cottages, known locally as 'The Tumbles', which feature as the setting for *Back to Basics*, the very popular ITV situation comedy of the 1980s. During the programme's six-year run, an estimated weekly audience of 17.3 million viewers sat enthralled to watch 'a commune of City commodities brokers and their families struggle to maintain their hectic careers and busy lifestyles, while courageously enduring the trials and tribulations of weekend self-sufficiency – with hilarious results' (*TV Listings*, Jun. 12-18, 1982). The buildings were only ever used for the occasional exterior scene, as in the title sequence when they appear to the accompanying strains of 'An English Country Garden', and had otherwise been neglected since the turn of the 20th century.

In the late-1960s, however, 'The Tumbles' were discovered by a radical free-spirited group calling themselves The Children of the Soil, who occupied the property until they were forced from the premises after the instigation of lengthy legal proceedings, by which time the buildings were 'in an advanced state of deterioration and consequently uninhabitable' (*WCC FINAL Eviction Notice*, Feb. 12, 1979). The cottages were acquired by Jerry Botchet & Sons following the liquidation of Paradise Productions in October 1988, but a preservation order prohibited 'the complete demolition and clearing of the site to allow development of an extensive sport and leisure complex' (*WCC Planning Permission Application no. 2897*, Apr. 3, 1989). Again the houses lay empty, but in August 1995, with the assistance of funding from the EU, 'The Tumbles' were finally restored to their former glory by Lovely Dream Homes Ltd, and a typical example is recently described as:

> Charmg Vic terrd bung, lux rest with many orig feats. Vest, hall, lnge, ftd kit/diningrm, 1 dbl bedrm/ens, 1 sgl bedrm, bathrm, CH/DG, lge rear gdn. Perf rural ret, 20 mins fm S'bury.
>
> Fleece & Co., *Monthly List* (Jun. 2004)

Originally, however, the houses were built for the tenants of Lord William St John Penbury, who unconventionally adopted his wife's family name when he remarried in 1866. William 'Bill' Hodges, or 'B.H.', as he liked to be known, spent much of his early life in the suburbs of Delhi in India, behind the high walls of an enormous colonial residence that belonged to his great-uncle Cedric (a collector of taxes for East India Company), which was later destroyed in the defeated Sepoy Mutiny of 1857. His father, Lord Albert Godfrey William St John Penbury, maintained the estate until 1860, when he was tragically killed by 'Drudge', the estate's gamekeeper, in a shooting accident, while his mother Lady Constance 'followed suit upon hearing the news' (Dr Albert Wiggins, *Letter to Lord Godfrey Penbury*, Aug. 14, 1860).

In 1856, William returned to England and took a bachelor apartment on the Strand in London where, by his own admission, he filled his days 'with little else to do but eat, sleep and drink' (William Penbury,

Letter to Charles 'Tubby' Tuppington, 13th Earl of Portlyvale, Jul. 21, 1857). He did, however, find time to secure a substantial fortune by investing part of his yearly allowance in a small-armaments factory, which was owned by a cousin in California, shortly before the outbreak of the American Civil War. He was married in a hastily arranged ceremony on June 13, 1863, but on the same day news arrived that his elder brother Lord Godfrey St John Penbury, a notorious gambler and womaniser, had recently passed away in mysterious circumstances during an extended business trip to Bristol. William sent word that he would 'return to manage the estate as soon as was humanly possible' (Lord William Penbury, *Letter to George Todd*, Jul. 15, 1863).

He arrived at the manor a month later with his first wife Elizabeth, who originally came from London where her father, the Marquis of Ormiston, was a great socialite and the owner of several Mayfair properties.

Having curtailed their honeymoon touring the delights of Europe, Lady Elizabeth withdrew from society and settled down to live a quiet life at the manor, although she did make medical history by becoming the first and, as yet, only person 'to contract syphilis by sharing the same pair of rose clippers with her decrepit and pox ridden gardener' (Dr Albert Wiggins, *Letter to Prof. J.J. Humerus FRCS*, Nov. 8, 1863). She died six weeks later at the age of 22.

At around this time many people in Britain were beginning to think that the benefits of the industrial revolution had been achieved at a great cost in human happiness. The living and working conditions of many were, to say the least, rotten. Another concern was that the traditional rhythms of life and the close relationship between human beings and the world that they inhabited had been irreversibly lost to progress.

Although initially disinterested in country life, preferring instead to spend much of his time in London, William seems to have sustained his grief by steadily immersing himself in the day-to-day running of the estate. Gradually he met each member of his workforce and, in turn, 'was delighted to be introduced to their many relations and friends' (Lord Penbury, *Diary*, March 13, 1864). He soon began to pride himself on his knowledge of country trades and farming implements, and was often surprised by what he calls his 'natural ability to perform a skilful task' (*ibid*).

The respected Prof. Jimmy Moffett of the Department of Social Policy with the Open University says:

> Hodges empathised with his workers to a point that was unthinkable within the ruling-class of Victorian society. Furthermore, this unique affiliation would transform one of England's most prominent aristocrats into perhaps the greatest radical freethinker of his generation and a stanch advocate of early communism and social reform. *Left Foot Forward* (1987)

In the beginning of 1864, having witnessed for himself 'the abominable conditions that were allowed to flourish under the previous landlord' (Rev. T. Flockhart, *Letter to Lord Penbury*, Jan. 10, 1864), William initiated an ambitious programme to rebuild and modernise the estate. His first act was to raise all wages by 15 per cent, a measure that he paid for from his own pocket. Existing properties were soon upgraded by improved sanitation, and when any worker's cottage housed more than eight in one room it was immediately enlarged to accommodate any possible new arrival. Interestingly, the parish records show that in 1864 there were a total of 438 people living on the Penbury estate. By 1870, that number had soared to 512.

In May 1865, William married Gwyneth Hodges who, over the next six years, provided him with three daughters, Marigold, Lily, Rose, and a son William, who survived for only an hour after he was born.

Bill Hodges, as he was now widely known, made it his duty to reverse what he seems to have agreed were 'the aberrant wrongs that have been perpetrated on the people of this parish' (*ibid*). As the Penbury estate was primarily a rural enterprise, working hours could not be altered, but the introduction of a fair rotation system provided welcome relief from strenuous or repetitive duties. From 1865, the employment of children was strictly regulated, and a year later every child under the age of 10 was obliged to attend to the newly established Hodges' School for the Formation of Character – a converted barn on the outskirts of Fritteringale.

When these basic reforms were in place the estate is understood to have achieved better results in production and trade, although precise documentary evidence in support of this has yet to emerge. By the turn of the decade, however, Hodges would claim to be 'presiding over the rudiments of an ideal model community in which', he boasts, 'workers and their families enjoy a privileged and rewarding existence that exceeds far and above that of their contemporaries' (Bill Hodges, 'Letter to the Editor', *Times Newspaper*, Jan. 29, 1870).

Hodges' efforts even secured royal approval during a visit to Wiltshire by the Prince of Wales, who was touring the area with local dignitaries and is reported to have replied '"most interesting" when he was asked to comment on the latest advancements' (*Salisbury Crier*, Apr. 13, 1872).

Hodges, however, did not simply delegate and oversee the development of the estate but actively participated in the work, preferring instead to 'Get Stuck In', as the grand inscription on the gatehouse vividly prescribes. He also organised regular social events and leisure activities for the enjoyment of his tenants. Hodges even revived the questionable 'Whip Lass' ritual, a customary 18th-century practice in which 'a chaste maiden is exhibited in familiar attitude and fought over by males of the parish with the assistance of ferocious rhubarb thrashing' (*Summer Fete Poster*, *c.* 1872).

Others, however, particularly the residents of the nearby village of Littlehoot, found the events 'rambunctious occasions', while the Harvest Festival in particular was singled out as 'nothing other than three days of licentious debauchery and riotous behaviour' (Rev. Thomas Twee, *Letter to Squire Pishwit*, Sep. 23, 1873).

Nevertheless, and undeterred by his critics, Hodges ploughed on with his arrangements and constantly sought ways to improve the lives of his 'charges', as he often refers to the people of the estate in his diary. He even maintained his famous Green Man or Jack-in-the-Green tradition, whereby, on the morning of each May Day, he would assume the attire of the mischievous guardian spirit of the ancient woodlands and parade through the estate's orchards – to be showered with apple blossom by adoring womenfolk – until the penultimate year of his life.

Hodges became a great benefactor and as well as providing 'a basket of choicest provisions to every dwelling each Michaelmas in receipt of the quarterly rent' (Lord Penbury, *Edict 28 to Mr George Todd*, Feb. 6, 1864), he also donated generously to many charitable causes.

Yet aside from these pioneering reforms as a landowner, Bill Hodges is equally well known for his passionate involvement in the arts and crafts movement, of which he not only amassed a considerable body of work, but also patronised many aspiring young artists by installing them in fashionable London accommodation. Hodges toured the length and breadth of British Isles in continuous search of evermore bucolic examples of painting, sculpture, ceramics, textiles and other items of objet d'art with which he took great delight in decorating his home. His interests extended to all manner of aesthetics, both ancient and modern, and soon broadened to include those of Europe, his beloved India, North Africa, and the Middle and Far East. When abroad, Hodges usually travelled at the head of a great entourage, which usually consisted of his entire family, a wide circle of friends and those domestic servants from the manor who could be spared. In addition, and in return for 'a small baksheesh', he was not above 'securing a local escort when arriving at a new destination and, if the company was particularly large, engage the services of several pack wallahs to lighten the burden and hasten the transportation of luggage' ('B.H.', *Diary*, Jul. 6, 1875). Hodges became increasingly fascinated by the specific art of particular region and would often write on the subject to his sister-in-law P.J. Trollop RSA, the famous water-colourist and a fellow artisan:

> Today, Sunday, I broke from our itinerary and toured the east of the city, where I was delighted to discover many beautiful objects, the quality of which would be difficult to replicate at home with the most modern equipment and manufacturing techniques, let alone the rudimentary tools of their maker.
>
> It was here that I sensed the real bond that exists between the noble craftsman and his

> creations, and, such is his concern that the unique and glorious nature of these items be preserved, I was cautioned to view them in the shade, least the vividness of their colour fade in the harsh sunlight. Furthermore, I was advised only to admire them in similar conditions while I remained in the district.
>
> 'B.H.', 'Cairo Street with Market', *Postcard* (Aug. 6, 1883)

Apart from these accumulative interests, Hodges was also a voracious essayist and prolific pamphleteer. He usually printed his work by hand in the south facing attic room of the manor, where he made his studio and produced such notable titles as *Art and the Masses* (1876), *The Philistine's Foibles* (1879) and the much sought after *Eastern Ecstasy* (1881), which, far from the title's suggestion, is actually an extensive mathematical inquiry that attempts to categorise the intricate patterns of Islamic tiling and fretwork.

He even published a slim volume of illustrated poetry that chronicles a year of life on the estate. The collection, which Hodges began in the spring of 1865, was favourably received by reviewers and elegantly described by one as 'earthy observations resplendently enthused with vivacious expressions of nature' (*Wiltshire Monthly Review* (Jul. 1883).

The Marriage

To Coffy Simms and Hetty Gumgrind
on their Wedding Day

Oh happy day! The world is gay
And all the birds are singing.
We'll rest and play, this month of May,
With all the joy it's bringing.
Yes, life is sweet when still we meet
With lovers pure and simple;
Our cares and woes, the common foes,
Would scarcely fill a thimble.

Ponderings from Penbury (1883)

Yet Hodges' best-known work is perhaps *Under the Sea* (1885), a fantastic tale about a futuristic 'world of equals' where oxygen is generated from seaweed and the entire populous carry heavy weights about their ankles, 'not to hinder their progress in life, but to prevent them ascending into the society of pirates and corruption that lies above'.

The Hollywood film *Aquarius* (1969) is loosely based on Hodges' novel and stars Vincent Gelbe as the brutish Captain Henry Spode in pursuit of Gloop Swithers, played by a boyish Jonathan Cummings, who is probably more familiar these days as the dashing gynaecologist Dr Byron Manly in the long-running US hospital drama *Intravenous Drip* (Utopia TV).

The film's opening battle sequence is perhaps the most impressive, but there is great attention to detail in the underwater scenes, particularly when the two adversaries descend unconscious into the deep and are rescued by the inhabitants of Globe City, the nation's capital.

After a brief audience before the Grand Council, Captain Spode and Swithers are thrown into adjacent cells of the city's notorious Clam Penitentiary, and there follows a humorous episode as the pair viciously goad and taunt each other through the dividing bars. Sir Anthony Treadboard is an inspired choice as the sadistic jailer, while Hob 'Hobby' Honk is unforgettable as his brainless but loyal sidekick. However, the set piece is ruined by a protracted flashback sequence in which Captain Spode pines for his absent sweetheart Esmeralda Grapple, who is inappropriately played by 'Babs, *Hots Magazine* April 1968, playmate-of-the-month' in an extravagant cameo appearance. The film regains some pace when Captain Spode finally escapes from his cell and, while hastening through the darkness of the city's complex ventilation system, he utters the famous line that he is later forced to recant: 'I will not live with these fish!'

Cummings is certainly miscast as the wealthy merchant, although Audrey Wendge in her first screen role gives a feisty performance as Comrade Sturgeon, who is charged with returning Captain Spode to Aquarius and preventing him revealing the country's secret location. The comedy duo The Double Entendres are afforded more than adequate licence as the two disgruntled gatekeepers, while Groovy George performs the contagious 'H_20', which he especially wrote for the production. As expected, the direction of Leslie 'the lens' Marshal is up to the usual high standard of his previous work, yet the overall effect is stale and Gelbe's talents are wasted in what became the final film of an illustrious career.

Although *Aquarius* performed well at the box-office, critics were divided on the film's merits between the predictable 'wet' (Justine Foggerty, *Cinema '69*, 1970), the scathing 'implausible and technically inaccurate' (*Scuba Magazine*, Jun. 1969), to the more enthusiastic 'swimming' (*Movies Weekly*, May 29, 1969). However, scholars of Hodges' work condemned 'the tenuous parallel with 1960's popular culture' and denounced 'the scandalous alteration of the book's ending', where Swithers instigates a failed rebellion and is banished from Aquarius without the aid of a respirator, to a war of attrition with surface ships from which the Aquarians eventually find refuge on an oceanic world in outer space (widely recognised as a subtle reference but an improbable conclusion to the ensuing conflict in Vietnam), as 'damn silly hippy hogwash' (Prof. J.G. Monsoon, 'Views from the Stalls', *Movies Weekly*, Jun. 5, 1969).

All the same, many audiences were suitably impressed by the then state-of-the-art special-effect wizardry that was required to bring the novel to the big screen, while no one could possibly forget the catchy tag-line of the film's trailer:

> Yes, you really will believe people can live under water for an indefinite period of time without the pressing requirement of cumbersome breathing apparatus.

Although the society envisaged in *Under the Sea* has never been successfully realised, and may even be dismissed as fanciful and hopelessly impractical, it does at least reflect Hodges' political aspirations that saw people living productive and fulfilled lives, away from poverty and fear, in an age when such things were denied to so many.

Hodges may have been a humanist at heart, but he was not without his spiritual side and was a great exponent of Hinduism, Buddhism and Islam, 'the exotic faiths' as he likes to call them in his diary. Occasionally he would return from abroad in the company of 'a moral advisor', whom he would install at the manor for 'an indefinite period to provided intuitive insight, invaluable guidance and constructive criticism, which has been noticeably thin on the ground of late' ('B.H.', *Diary*, Aug. 16, 1891).

Hodges also showed a brief interest in the paranormal, during which time the famous medium Andre Blotch was invited to hold a monthly seance at the HSFC. The events proved popular, but they were eventually curtailed when Blotch was 'exposed as a fraudulent trickster by the Duchess of Shrewsbury and awarded five years of hard labour for his crimes, to the obvious approval of the London High Court's public gallery' (*Times Newspaper*, Feb. 10, 1892).

Hodges even made several excursions into mystical and, through the influence of such memorable characters as 'Wise Mary' and 'The Soothsayer', who visited the estate on the winter and summer solstice respectively, he gained the dubious reputation as 'some sort of swami who attains regular success when dousing for water' (Arthur Todd, *Letter to Squire Pishwit*, Nov. 13, 1894).

As well as demonstrating a vibrant passion for numerology, astrology and cosmology, Hodges was also an eminent member of the Druids and officiated at many of their ceremonies, which is perhaps less surprising given the manor's location, believed to be resting on the crossing of ancient ley lines roughly 10 km north of Stonehenge.

Sadly, however, on the evening of December 31, 1899, 'towards the end of an otherwise enjoyable evening of dinner, song and merriment, Hodges collapsed while attempting to demonstrate an act of physical prowess before the ladies' ('Obituary', *Times Newspaper*, January 2, 1900).

Shortly after the house and grounds were acquired by the War Department and incorporated into the military training area on Salisbury Plain. Subsequently, nothing but the foundations of the manor remain, although the gatehouse, outwith the designated site, still stands and is now owned by the British Heritage Society.

A few years ago, while surveying what remains of this building, Sir Reginald Bland, the famous architect and celebrated authority on mid-Victorian brick and stonemasonry, discovered 'hidden in the oversized chimney stack, among some glorious demonstrations of multifarious herringbone and crosshatching arrangements, a tin box emblazoned with the monogram "B.H." and a badly scorched bundle of papers therein. The box was regrettably lost during the inspection of a dilapidated drainage system, where it may still be found along with a beige overcoat, *The Architects' Association Diary 1997*, a novelty fountain pen and an inexpensive but rather attractive pigskin wallet that contained several major credit cards, a return ticket to London and at least £60 in cash' (Sir Reginald Bland, *Letter to Edward Fens, S Eng. Dir. BHS*, Apr. 30, 1997).

It appears that following Hodges' death the estate quickly fell into disrepair and many workers moved from the area in search of alternative employment. The tiny village of Fritteringale, 'My Eden', as Hodges refers to the protectorate in his diary, was soon abandoned and the buildings were later demolished to make way for army personnel housing shortly after the Second World War.

Why the Penbury estate should deteriorate in such an alarming manner is uncertain, but as there was no apparent evidence of Hodges' intentions, the family and senior estate members evidently presumed that he had died intestate and immediately engaged in jealous squabbles over the inheritance.

The papers that were found by Sir Reginald were immediately sent to the family's solicitors, formerly Jessop, Jessop, Jessop & Co., a prestigious Salisbury firm that has recently amalgamated with the highly successful *www.easypeasylemonadesqueezy.co.uk*.

Intense publicity surrounded the discovery of the documents, as it was hoped that they might reveal the whereabouts of the family's missing fortune – recorded at £932,184 by Mr Arbuthnot Jessop in September 1899, and which, if prudently invested, would amount to several millions today. On the afternoon of May 5, 1997, in a suite at the Savoy Hotel in London, with an expectant media scum waiting impatiently outside, the surviving relatives of those named on the title sheet assembled before senior partners of the afore-mentioned company and eagerly anticipated the contents of the following manuscript.

The document is undated, unsigned and possibly intended as an early draft.

Last Will and Testament
of
Bill Hodges, Penbury Manor, Wiltshire

I, Bill Hodges, formally Lord William St John Penbury, being of sound mind, body and spirit (a condition that I wholeheartedly attributed to a simple diet of root vegetables, dairy produce and the daily ritual of labour, leisure and studied contemplation in alignment with the cosmos), do hereby make my last will and testament.

I commit my soul to the Empyrean and my Creator.

In accordance with my instructions to Mr Todd, our trusted steward, my body is to be placed in a cuboid casket of my own design and decoration – with legs and arms akimbo. Following a simple ceremony, the agenda of which I have recently entrusted to our young Rev. Flockhart, the box should be centred in the family vault, which should be completed as soon as sufficient quantities of Grecian iron oak and Egyptian basalt arrive to grace the interior. (This, I am reliably informed by the builders' merchants Grabbit Bros. of Trowbridge, should be any day now.)

To my beloved wife Gwyneth, 'Gwinny', my Guinevere and tireless companion. I am reminded of the day we met, for what chance it was that such a rarity as you should be thrown from her horse, to land like a windfall petal at my feet, during my compulsory twice-yearly visit to our lawyers in Salisbury. As I listened to your tale of despair in the Cross Keys Hotel, I vowed to myself that you would never again return to your miserable existence in Bristol. Our beloved house, its contents and the entire estate of Penbury are yours, my dear. I have every confidence that (regardless of recent advances made by gentlemen from the government, and with the assistance of Mr Todd with whom you did so enjoyably collaborate in supervising work on the folly when I was regrettably bedridden last spring) the affairs of our little community are assured.

As I have woefully failed in my duty to secure suitable husbands for my three daughters, they will of course remain at their mother's side and continue to assist, as they have always done, in the financial administration of our enterprise.

Boosaki, dear Boosaki, my faithful manservant, confidant and friend. It is my greatest regret that I may never visit your home village set, I am told, among lush pastures beneath the foothills of the Sahara. I can only hope that our frugal offerings to your people over these past few years have in some small way assisted in their constant battle against the deadly plagues of Swonga ant that regularly blight their lives. You, Sir, shall be my executor.

Lastly, but by no means least, Mr Todd. Your father was a great solace to me in the early years of my overlord. George Todd was a man of the soil, thoroughly honourable and solely responsible for steering me from my previous life of indolence and fancy. It was George Todd and his dear wife Marigold for whom I built the gatehouse and removed them, somewhat bewildered, from their wretched cottage on the river. I was afforded the greatest pleasure to watch your dear parents live out their days in return for a nominal rent that, try as I might, I could never refuse. Mr Todd, for as long as you remain steward of the Penbury estate, which I am confident will be for many years to come, despite the interest expressed in the property by our insensible neighbour (who shall remain nameless), the house is yours in which to live. It may also interest you to know that before the gatehouse was completed, I hid a small token of appreciation to your parents under the floorboards of the lady's drawing room should it ever be required.

Extensive excavations of the gatehouse only succeeded in reducing the building to a ruined shell, although Sir Reginald was eventually reunited with his novelty fountain pen.

The final irony is that although Hodges dismissed his peerage as ‘a worthless trinket’ and shunned any benefits that it may have granted him through what he saw as ‘the twin evils of influence and privilege’ (‘B.H.’, *Diary*, Jan. 1, 1866), he deeply regretted the loss of his son, who might have continued to maintain and reform the estate when he was no longer able. The Penbury estate may have failed in Hodges’ absence but, with no male heir to succeed him, the title also died with His Lordship.

‘Honest Terms’

(pending release)

Still basking in the critical acclaim of his recently published autobiography, *My Septic Isle* (Ewing Press, 2004), an illustration in stark realism of 16 traumatic years of brutal detention at HM Prison Parkhurst that cumulates in a desperate plea for prison reform, the irrepressible Stilton Croker, a.k.a. ‘Cheese Wire’, accomplished painter, sculptor, writer, poet and audacious raconteur, is currently compiling a modest compendium of many useful words and phrases that may be unfamiliar to those about to re-enter society.

A brief preview of the work in progress appears below and, evidently drawn from personal experience, subtly demonstrates the ex-offender’s predicament when attempting to integrate with an ever-changing and often hostile world after a prolonged period of forced and indignant exile.

Honest Terms, the title is rumoured, seeks to end society’s abhorrent discrimination of the previously incarcerated and empower the disaffected with a renewed confidence through the acquisition of a wide and varied vocabulary that is eminently suitable for any company.

Croker’s selfless endeavour promises to make fascinating reading and will undoubtedly prove an invaluable resource for prison officials, parole officers and others working in the profession, while poignantly highlighting a shameful oversight by the Home Office in adequately preparing inmates for life in the community.

Honest Terms

aromatherapy a pure tonic; a godsend.

Artex (tdmk) some indication of the previous generation's sense of taste.

beeswax a superb wood preservative with the remarkable ability to hide a multitude of sins.

bicurious obviously people with too much time on their hands.

Buddhist a lover of bright clothes, tambourine music and colouring books – usually bald.

Cabernet Sauvignon a uniformly successful grape variety, adored by winemakers for producing a delightful and full-bodied 'red', the playfulness of which never fails to amuse.

conservatory an oasis of sanity where quiet moments of contemplation may be enjoyed, gloriously alleviating the tiresome but inevitable stress of modern life.

domestic a small, very rare gem from the Far East.

dyslexia an inconsequential phenomenon, extremely common among gifted children.

e-mail such a trial to keep abreast of, but just another one of those things one cannot possibly live without these days.

ethnic passé.

feng shui see *interior design.*

ginseng oriental tea that contains medicinal and, some would say, even mystical properties.

hashish the correct term for the old 'Jim Jones', 'Maryanne' or 'Oliver Reed', a harmless and socially acceptable recreational drug that ought to be legalised if only to help alleviate the pain and suffering of MS.

herbaceous border a pleasure to the eye and a joy to the senses.

interior design an absolute must.

kitsch such fun in moderation.

loft conversion worthy of serious consideration that will enhance and significantly increase the value of any property.

loss adjuster a thief immune from prosecution.

minimalist was it not Browning who said 'less is more'?

nostalgia a misplaced loyalty for outmoded business practice; a liability.

orthodontics extortion by means of emotional blackmail.

postmodern new... ish.

PTSD (post-traumatic stress disorder) depression suffered after a horrifying ordeal, particularly common among commuters in the south-east of England.

RSI (repetitive strain injury) a windfall.

SAD (seasonal affective disorder) a shameful excuse for habitual absenteeism.

single currency (vulg.) a dirty word (actually two, to be pedantic) in specific houses; the flagrant erosion of one's national identity.

singleton a disrupter of seating arrangements, but an exceptionally fine malt whisky all the same.

SMS (short message service, also *text message*) another language in the opinion of most people, totally incomprehensible to anyone over the age of 12.

tagliatelle so versatile with a little imagination and a much-maligned source of protein and carbohydrate.

web-site a bloody goldmine if you ask Trevor.

woodchip wallpaper a demonstration of ignorance.

xenophobia simply a question of standards.

Yuletide the proper name for Christmas.

zed what Shakespeare called 'thou unnecessary letter'.

Reproduced with the gracious permission of S. Croker.

Communal Statements

Fog everywhere. Charles Dickens, *Bleak House* (1883)

On June 15, 1970, an article entitled 'Pop Goes the Weasel' appeared in the late edition of the *Daily Courier* telling of 'an explosion' on the previous Sunday in a small lodging house on the Kennington Road in Lambeth. There were no fatalities but 'some injuries' are reported, and the building, 'now in severe danger of collapse', was ordered to be evacuated by officers of the London Fire Brigade. Readers are further told that 'the property may have to be demolished, but only after a thorough examination is carried out to determine the exact cause of the blast.'

The only casualty, it seems, was a tame stoat called Treacle, who usually occupied the outside lavatory but was given run of the house by the landlord, 'often', the article informs, 'to the consternation of residents and prospective tenants alike, as the conspicuous notice in the parlour window advertising "Rooms to Let" specifically states "No children, pets or Irish".'

The item says that 'the explosion was confined to the rear of the building, with the hallway, stairwell and rooms to the front suffering only minor damage, but the kitchen, scullery and washroom were less fortunate, and several rooms on the first and second floor were devastated.' The article goes on to say that 'furniture, household items and personal belongings were blown into the yard, and part of the exterior wall had collapsed with Treacle, in the outhouse below, fielding most of the debris.'

The story was ignored by the rest of the media, whose members were perhaps otherwise engaged with coverage of the forthcoming general election. However, a brief passage in the ever inventive *South London Crier* (Jun. 18, 1970), which was then running a virulent anti-smoking campaign, pre-empts the eventual findings of the official investigation and concludes that 'the occurrence was obviously caused by an accumulation of methane gas in the decrepit Victorian sewer below the building, and was probably ignited by a carelessly discarded cigarette.'

Extensive repairs were made to the property and the sewer was completely renovated, but when it emerged that the sole contractor of the work was Capital Constructions Ltd, 'We Get it Right First Time', a firm headed by Councillor Gerald Dooley, brother-in-law of Harold 'the Hose' Hewitt, a senior divisional officer with the London Fire Brigade whose recommendations had been accepted by the Borough Council, all assumptions were thrown into question. Furthermore, when additional revelations came to light concerning 'similar incidents of Hewitt's alleged impropriety', the authorised report was condemned as 'the product of greed and shameless corruption' (*South London Crier*, Jul. 9, 1970).

Intriguingly, on August 13, 1981, the same paper ran a small advert in its personal column on behalf of

Messrs Twee, Futtock and Smime, who were seeking relatives of the late Jacob 'Joby' Grimbold, a former police constable and lifelong resident of the Lambeth area. The immediate response is said to have been 'phenomenal, far exceeding all expectations' (Geoffrey Twee, Randolph Futtock and Jeremy Smime, *Letter to Chief Constable Steven Ballard*, Aug. 14, 1981). In addition, the partners go on to say that:

> ... on the day that the advert appeared several hundred people swamped our usually quiet office and, as we were completely unprepared for the onslaught, most were forced to stand in the corridor, on the stairs or wait outside on the pavement in heavy rain.
>
> Understandably many became irritable and, in frustration, possibly invaded the premises of our fellow tenants, during which time some theft and the destruction of property may have occurred.

All the same, when it emerged that apart from a few personal effects the estate amounted to nothing, and that the purpose of the exercise was to find a benefactor willing to cover Mr Grimbold's prearranged funeral expenses, all but one abandoned their claim.

Ernest Proberty was the librarian of Lambeth Public Library, an amateur sociologist and perhaps a professional acquaintance of PC Grimbold.

Before his employment with Lambeth Council Proberty's early life is something of a mystery. It has been assumed that he was 'the illegitimate son of the notorious East-End spiv Norman “Knuckles” Norton, whose brutal reign of terror ended in a bloodbath with the dominant Steptoe brothers at the home of his former mistress on February 14, 1956 (Charlie ‘Chopper’ Chapman, ‘Wos Yor Game, Ay?’, *’Ard Men o’ London*, ed. Prof. S.R. Banners, 1985). Yet evidence has recently emerged that finds Norton ‘severely deficient in the downstairs department and hardly ever up to the job’ (Hilda Dribble, ‘The Dry Years: 1939-45’, *On the Game: The Diaries of London’s Prostitutes*, ed. Marjory Baxter. 1999).

Additionally, on his birth certificate Elsie Proberty’s son is named Eustace Oliver Proberty, after her father and uncle respectively, which sheds more doubt on Ernest’s origin, while Norton, regardless of his supposed shortcomings, is said to have ‘repeatedly demanded a boy to name after and keep control of what he called “va bizniz”’ (*ibid*).

Fascinatingly, the nature of Proberty’s relationship with PC Grimbold is possibly recorded in Horace Greebling’s famous pub guide *Solitary Boozers* (1971). This delightful companion does not, as the title implies, illustrate the insular habits of the lone drinker, but instead attempts ‘to extol the virtues of the free house over the many powerful and faceless conglomerates’ that were, in Greebling’s opinion, ‘encroaching upon the industry in pursuit of profit with complete disregard for customer satisfaction or local heritage’. However, Greebling’s obvious passion for his subject, coupled with an unwavering desire to preserve the past, may be responsible for a tendency to cloud his accounts of some of London's less salubrious public houses. For instance, the entry below refers to a stark utilitarian building that once stood on waste ground near the Elephant and Castle. The building, which was no more that a large shelter, was initially a motor mechanic's garage before its procurement as a collection point and temporary storage facility for Lord Beverbrook's many salvage drives that took place during the Second World War. His Lordship's repeated demands for scrap iron and aluminium were often reported as 'thoroughly successful affairs in which everyone in the country could contribute' (*Times Newspaper*, Jul. 30, 1940). However, such measures were primarily designed as a propaganda exercise to raise morale on the home front, while their benefits to the war effort remain questionable. Indeed, much of what was gathered in Lambeth remained piled high at the rear of The Traveller's Rest for several years and eventually became what the chairman of the local residents' committee would call 'a grotesque blot on the landscape and a haven for gypos on the scavenge' (Ronald Bleat, *Letter to Cr Gerald Dooley*, Oct. 27, 1971). Nevertheless, for Horace Greebling, who often spent 'many a happy evening propping up the bar in complete admiration of Miss Armstrong's vocational aptitude, or perhaps lounging by the fire engaged in yet another round of uproarious Cockney parlance', the building was 'a blissful refuge to be regularly patronised by all manner of local colour'.

Greebling continues:

At around six o'clock on this fine autumnal day I found myself heading down St George's Road, where I stumbled upon (by accident I might add and not as a result of my moderate mid-day libation at The Pig and Whistle) an oasis of merriment that is officially listed as The Traveller's Rest, but known locally as the 'Dog and Duck'.

I felt as if some guiding hand had led me to the door of these glorious premises, for, set among ungracious surroundings that do no credit to its architectural splendour, this particular south of the river hostelry must surely be one of the best kept secrets in London.

As the 'George Bernard' swung silently behind me, all present turned towards the mysterious 'Glasgow Ranger' who was adjusting his 'pork pies' to the evening sunlight that was flooding in through the partially glazed and boarded 'cinder'.

After a moment's apprehension, which, as I have said many times before, is a perfectly natural sensation that even the most seasoned professional will experience, I overcame my anxiety and, ignoring the muted 'rabbit' that was emanating from the two 'Hillman Hunters' seated at the 'Betty Grable' in the 'Jack Horner', strode purposefully towards the 'Tommy Farr'.

As is my custom when entering unknown and perhaps even hazardous territory, the 'tiddlies' were on me, and I proffered a crisp new 'Lady

Godiva' for a pint of 'chalky white', a 'runner and rider', a large 'Tom Thumb', a 'bright and frisky', a small 'Vera Lynn' and a packet of 'will o' the wisps', while giving every indication to the officiating 'lemon squeezer' that I would not require the 'kitchen'.

My initial reception was mixed, while Danny, who later became a firm friend and godfather to our youngest grandchild, did not even thank me for the 'sherbet', but instead returned indifferently to his 'skyscraper' in which he was studying the form of the evening's 'cherries'.

As time wore on, however, and I found myself once more indulging in a rather expensive but particularly fine 'Woolwich Ferry' (the name of which I am unable to remember, having never encountered the article before nor since), I began to feel quite at home in my discovery and, with subsequent visits and a little persistence, eventually became acquainted with some of the 'rubber's' early evening regulars.

On one occasion I remember pulling up a 'Vanity Fair' beside Frankie 'Fingers' Frompton, or 'F', as I was permitted to call him, a petty 'tea leaf' and habitual 'Harold Macmillan'.

Over the discarded remains of an uninspiring game of 'Wilkie Bards', we were discussing the likelihood of decimalisation (and the benefits that it might bring to his profession) when in walked a 'bottle top' on the 'duck and dive'. I later learned that the officer in question was familiarly known as 'Joby' and, my companion informed me, was thoroughly 'Duke of Kent' and a real 'bread and butter'. I further discovered that the 'Dog and Duck' is not only a blissful refuge for the connoisseur of life's pleasures, but also a hive of industry in which the exchange of a little contraband is not unusual. The accommodating proprietors Vince and Molly Adams, a devoted couple of some thirty years standing, generally turn a blind eye to the practice, yet such activities invariably attract attention from the local 'Beechams'.

'Joby' calmly surveyed the premises with an air of disapproval, while Nobby Wort left him grimacing in the 'pen and ink' of a strident 'raspberry tart', which he fearlessly blew as he walked passed the officer on his way to the 'cat and dog' for a 'two bob bit'.

'Joby', undeterred by the atmosphere of hostility that he had encountered, saddled up beside one of the 'rubber's' more reserved patrons, a gentleman of fervent delicacy who is known in the vicinity as 'Probes'.

In all honesty you could never meet a more timorous fellow, yet 'Joby', a great 'lump of coke', gratuitously punched him in the 'orchestra stalls', kicked him out the 'George Bernard' and down the 'field of wheat'. Over the coming months I was pleased to see 'Probes' again inhabit his usual 'boiled sweet' in the 'Dog and Duck', however, on each occasion he bore an increasingly sombre countenance about his ‘boat race’ and was usually sporting a fresh set of bruises.

It is to the detriment of such innocuous taverns like the ‘Dog and Duck’ when decent souls attempting to enjoy a moment’s relaxation (or perhaps conduct some harmless business transaction) are prevented from doing so by abominable interference from the loutish ‘Uncle Wilf’.

In November 1971, the Traveller’s Rest is said to have ‘succumbed to the action of wrecking ball with stubborn defiance (Horace Greebling, *Solitary Boozers*, 2nd ed. 1973), although the managing director of the company that was contracted to clear the site had previously judged the operation ‘no trouble at all’ (Cr Gerald Dooley, *Letter to Ronald Bleat*, Oct. 29, 1971).

While fascinating in its own right, Greebling’s account of ‘Probes’ does not sit easily with those of others who have encountered Ernest Proberty – if indeed they are the same person. Additional records relating to the weakling ‘Probes’ have yet to surface, but extensive enquires have been made of Ernest Proberty to reveal a character that is less than virtuous.

Under the pseudonym ‘Gordon Gromwit’, Proberty published a string of spurious survival pamphlets during the Cold War. These ‘twisted communications’, it is said, ‘pervade nothing but harmful and contradictory information, to the detriment of an admittedly loyal but misguided readership and solely conducive to the pocket of the accused' (Sir James Kilgour, *Crown v Proberty*, Jul. 1963). During his three day trial at the Old Bailey, Proberty is reported to have 'pleaded his innocence and defended himself with great eloquence' (*Times Newspaper*, Aug. 1, 1963), although a majority of the jury thought otherwise and secured him six months in prison.

Proberty was released on parole in January 1964 and not only managed to resume work for his former employer, but was actually promoted to the post of head librarian within three months of his return. Stranger still was that, under the same name and contrary to the terms of his release, Proberty persisted in producing other misleading and inaccurate leaflets, although their popularity had long since diminished.

In the late-1960s, however, with a fresh issue on the boil, Proberty re-emerged with such inflammatory titles as 'Britain under the Harvest Moon' (May 1968), 'The Pot of Glue Runneth Over' (Jul. 1968) and the equally controversial 'One Ounce of Baccy per Street' (Aug. 1968). These and other malicious brochures tried to capitalise on the prevailing mood of racial prejudice that flourished within Britain following Enoch Powell's infamous 'River Tiber foaming with much blood' speech, in which the then Conservative MP warned of the possible problems that might arise from unrestricted immigration.

Although Proberty's sentiments found some support with the public, particularly when a letter of his appeared in the *Times Newspaper* (Jun. 14, 1968) advocating 'compulsory Christian worship for people of all faiths who reap the benefits of their adopted country yet persist in their refusal to call themselves British', the theological community was less enthusiastic.

In an article that appears in the Easter edition of a monthly broadsheet, written and published by disaffected members of the Church of England, Proberty claims that 'the Vatican must surely be home to all manner of miscreants and ne'er-do-wells who are no doubt continually engaged in libidinous acts of sexual depravity' (Ernest Proberty, 'Papist Poppycock', *The Pulpit*, Mar. 1969). Furthermore, he not only claims that 'Pope Paul VI is in all probability a homosexual', but goes on to say that 'the Catholic faith is undoubtedly responsible for everything that is wrong with the country today, from over 1000 years of history to the weather outside.' Fortunately for the Church of Rome, however, the substance of Proberty's reasoning is dismissed as 'tenuous', while the article itself is condemned for its 'chronic historical inaccuracies and sweeping generalisations' (Fr Shamus O'Brien, 'Sing Out, Readers!' *The Pulpit*, Apr. 1969).

The only other account of Proberty's early life to emerge so far is found in the *Times Newspaper* (Sep. 1, 1958) and resides among similar reports from Notting Hill. Readers are informed of:

> ... a fracas between residents of the Ladbroke Grove and some disgruntled former tenants who were returning to the area from national service.

> A police spokesman said: 'reasonable force had been reluctantly deployed to quell the disturbance', although the source did admit that many people had required hospital treatment as a direct result of police intervention.
>
> Mr Ernest Proberty, a former private in the Royal Artillery, who claimed that he had innocently found himself in the thick of the fray, was asked to comment on the event and replied simply: 'They started it!'

In the first part of his best-selling autobiography *Up From the Ashes* (1997), the disgraced Conservative MP for Uppingworth South, Cuthbert Wilmington-Foss, recalls standing for the seat of Lambeth, Brixton during the 1970 general election. Regrettably, and at his first attempt to enter politics, the former quantity surveyor lost his deposit and came third behind an independent candidate who was representing 'a new and formidable force in British politics' (*Purity Party Manifesto*, 1970). Initially, Wilmington-Foss regarded Ernest Proberty as 'well rehearsed but a bit of a crackpot and certainly no match on the hustings for a prize-winning debater from Cambridge'. Nevertheless, when the final result was announced, following a campaign that, according to Wilmington-Foss, 'had occasionally verged on the disagreeable', the defeated Tory candidate was forced to concede that 'Proberty was not only popular with disheartened voters from both ends of the political spectrum, but also a master of disinformation.'

After the return of the successful Labour candidate, Proberty's interest in politics seems to have dwindled. However, in December 1995, he was called before the newly established Parliamentary Select Committee on Standards and Privileges, whereupon he was asked to explain his relationship with the Honourable Member for Uppingworth South who, along with three others, was facing questions for failing to disclose a part-interest in Proberty's thriving telephone introduction agency. Further investigations revealed that the enterprise secured its business by diverting calls from an obscure telephone in the Palace of Westminster to an unsavoury address in Bayswater. The affair became known as the infamous 'Tartgate' fiasco and ended the political careers of Wilmington-Foss and his co-accused. All others thought to be involved were investigated by the Director of Public Prosecutions, but when the true scale of the operation emerged, legal proceedings were dropped on the grounds of cost.

Ernest Proberty's present whereabouts are uncertain, although he is thought to have been the co-founder of, and a regular contributor to, the rarely visited *www.freelollypopstoys&asurprise.net*, the forerunner of today's very popular *www.iwont2csumpupyz.com*.

In August 1981, however, Proberty's business aspirations were more modest – although evidently no less mercenary.

Shortly after Proberty secured Joseph Grimbold's estate, some of the items appeared on display in Lambeth Public Library where, under the heading 'A Policeman's Lot', they were exhibited for over a year complete with a visitor's book and collection tin. Comments in the book range from the complimentary sentiments of Mrs M. Simmons of Lollard Street, who describes the presentation as 'one way to fill five minutes on a wet afternoon in March', to the disparaging 'Bollocks' from Mr H. Windsor on the Blackfriar's Road.

On October 14, 1982, PC Harold Winter and WPC Elsie Grey were called to a disturbance at the library in which Gerry O'Rourke, a resilient down-and-out and ravenous borrower, had accosted Dorothy Bored, a part-time member of staff, in an argument over outstanding fines. O'Rourke was escorted from the building without resistance and no further action was taken, but the two constables must have shown more than a passing interest in the library's modest exhibition as all articles on display were later confiscated by officers from Scotland Yard.

News of the incident found its way to the *Morning Dispatch*, which had annihilated the *South London Crier* during a bitter circulation war in November 1981. On October 15, 1982, under the sensational headline 'POLICE SEIZE GRIMBOLD DIARIES', the paper reports that 'among the items removed was a large leather bound volume recording the events of Joseph Grimbold's personal and professional life from January 1975 to his retirement from the force in August 1979.'

Furthermore, within a lengthy article that advocates 'freedom of information', while robustly arguing against what the paper's editorial calls 'this country's archaic laws of censorship', readers are also informed that 'in addition to the one confiscated from the library, an undisclosed number of similar volumes were removed from the home of Head Librarian Ernest Proberty.'

At the time Proberty was in the process of negotiating with the *Sunday Enquirer* to have the diaries serialised, but although police intervention ruined the venture, doubts had already been raised that the diaries may have been 'doctored for the sake of gratuitous sensationalism' (Sylvia Stevens, *Memo to Features Editor Harold Blat*, Sep. 27, 1982).

All eight of the *Grimbold Diaries* were held by Scotland Yard until some time shortly before January 1988, when they were sadly destroyed – apparently mistaken for vital evidence in the forthcoming appeal of the Birmingham Six (*Anonymous Source*).

In the summer of 1990, Proberty fled his home on Fitzalan Street following what one neighbour describes as 'an unholy racket that broke out in the early hours of Sunday morning, when an angry mob stormed the house and removed the landlord's daughter Josie, seven, from the building' (*Morning Dispatch*, Aug. 14, 1990). The paper also records that 'the rooms were ransacked', and Proberty's belongings were 'plundered, smashed or thrown out into the street and burnt'. However, among Proberty's effects that escaped this insurgence, a single sheet of handwritten paper was found that appears to have been removed from a foolscap volume.

The writing has been analysed by the eminent

graphologist Claudia Monk and, although uncertain, is reported to compare favourably with other examples by the late Joseph Grimbold.

> ... arrived a[t] va building a[t] abou[t] six o'clock, whereupon I wi[t]nessed a scene ov such devastation va like ov which I ave never encoun[t]ered in over fir[t]y years on va force. I[t] reminded me ov one morning during va Blitz when I ad occasion to visi[t] Aun[t] Ger[t]rude, only to discover va[t] va entire ouse ad been hobli[t]era[t]ed, while dear Ger[t]ie, as I used to call er, slumbered peaceably in er bed.
>
> Ere, owever, I wos me[t] by Mr Arry Wong, a sprigh[t]ly gen[t]leman in is mid-seven[t]ies, who hoccupied va two adjoining rooms in va ha[tt]ic.
>
> Mr Wong informed me va[t] a sudden chill in va hair ad driven im ou[t] to va corner shop for a fresh can ov fuel for is paraffin ea[t]er. Ee furver said va[t] ee ad eard raised voices downstairs abou[t] alf an our hafore. Va only over fing ee could remember wos waking up soaking we[t] in va bafroom two floors direc[t]ly below.
>
> Mr Jock McPherson, a canny Sco[t] ov hinordina[t]e rotundity, wos si[tt]ing stunned by va kerbside. Ee too ad eard va earlier disturbance bu[t] turned is wireless up to drown ou[t] va noise. Ee distinc[t]ly remembers higni[t]ing va gas fire in is room wiv va same match va[t] ad previously li[t] is pipe. Owever, ee did admi[t] to

falling in[t]o a deep repose shor[t]ly after, cour[t]esy ov is evening toddy. Va gen[t]leman wos unable to helucida[t]e furver.

I ven approached an awai[t]ing hambulance, wherein Mr and Mrs Kaunda, who ren[t]ed va double room on va second floor, were being consoled a[t] va rear ov va vehicle wiv steaming mugs ov o[t] swee[t] tea. Boaf recall earing va dispu[t]e bu[t] claimed vay wos dishin[t]erested in va ma[tt]er being overwise hengaged.

La[t]er, Mr Kaunda wos in va po[tt]ing shed in search ov a formidable hinstrumen[t] to unearf somefing va[t] ee ad found buried in va back garden near a successful row ov charlo[tt]es. Mrs Kaunda, meanwhile, ad just popped upstairs for a momen[t] leaving a pan ov liver and honions sizzling on va ki[t]chen's troublesome gas stove. Mr Kaunda wos found by va hambulance crew, bruised and badly shaken, behind va compost eap, which ad apparen[t]ly shielded im from va blast, while Mrs Kaunda wos astonished to regain consciousness in va harms ov Mr Wong. Neiver, owever, could provide additional hinformation.

Claude Dupon[t], a flamboyan[t] Gaul and abi[t]ual smoker ov hexo[t]ic tobaccos, ad been relaxing in is room on va first floor, where ee wos hen[t]ertaining a young lady friend named Beryl Goodbody.

Va couple confirmed va[t] vere ad been an hargumen[t] a[t] va fron[t] door a[t] around five o'clock, alvough boaf chose to ignore va hou[t]burst. M. Dupon[t] believed va[t] i[t] might[t] ave ad somefing to do wiv va helection, bu[t] said va[t] as ee wos no[t] a Bri[t]ish ci[t]izen ee wos dishin[t]erested in such fings.

A[t] abou[t] five fir[t]y, M. Dupon[t] wos required to visi[t] va bafroom, bu[t] when ee discovered va[t] i[t] wos hoccupied ee urried down stairs to va hou[t]ouse. Once ee ad relieved imself, M. Dupon[t] remembered frowing away is cigare[tt]e as ee walked towards Mr Kaunda, who wos se[tt]ling down to an ard-earned rest aving just prised up a large me[t]al hobject from va soil.

M. Dupon[t] said va[t] va blast ad frown im fousands ov fee[t] in[t]o va hair, where ee remained for several ours in hadmiration ov all va pre[tt]y colours. Against is insistence, I declined to question im furver.

Miss Goodbody said va[t] she ad remained in M. Dupon[t]'s room, where she ad slept froughou[t] va entire even[t] and wos only awoken when fire hofficers broke down va door.

Finally, I encoun[t]ered Mr Manny Cohen, who ad just returned eavily bandaged from va local ospi[t]al. Alvough Mr Cohen confirmed va[t] vere ad been some disturbance a[t] va fron[t] door, ee could no[t] comprehend i[t]s nature, nor did ee fink i[t] appropria[t]e to get involved.

Alf an our la[t]er, ee wos under va stairs, among many cans ov pain[t] and bo[tt]les ov

> finner, in search ov firiegh[t]ers wiv a candle. As ee returned to va lounge, va blast knocked im off is fee[t] and blew im down va all. Ee described va even[t] as 'a most distressing experience', bu[t] refused to say more until ee ad fully recovered wiv wha[t] ee could salvage from va ruins a[t] is sister's ouse in Golders Green.

Apart from the landlord Alfred Collins, who was visiting an unknown lady friend in Peckham, and the popular character actor Amal Gupta, who rented the front bedroom on the third floor but was in hospital undergoing a severe hernia operation, the statements above account for all occupants of the building.

Police estimate the time of the explosion to be somewhere between 5.31pm at the earliest and 5.33pm at the very latest. The exact whereabouts of Treacle during these vital two minuets are unknown. No trace of the animal was ever found.

'Words of Wisdom'

from the book of Half-Truths

3.1 A short while ago, in a quiet and peaceful land where there was never any trouble and often little to do, there lived a man whose name (for the sake of argument) was Amos, and he had two sons called... Yule and... Voles.

2 Yule was the good son who always listened to his father and obeyed his every word. Voles, on the other hand, was the bad son who generally ignored the advice of his father and, given the slightest opportunity, would openly contradict him for no other reason than he knew that it infuriated Amos beyond belief. Consequently, there were times when Amos secretly wished that one of them had never been born at all.

3 Now, the day came for Yule and Voles to leave the home of their father and make their own way in the world. Amos, who had watched his sons grow from boys into men over the years with no thought of anything in return, was sorry but, at the same time, somewhat relieved to see them go.

4 Shortly before the appointed hour, Amos gathered the beloved fruit of his loins (and the other one) before him and provisioned them equally with all manner of necessities (and some inappropriate trifles) for the journey ahead. Then he said to his two sons, My dear

boys (Amos always referred to Yule and Voles as my dear boys, a comforting address that concealed the fact that one of them he did not like very much).

5 My dear boys, he said again (probably to emphasise the point), the days of your youth are expired, and you must go now forth from this place into a strange and wonderful realm that is the world outwith your home.

6 Having stated the obvious, Amos spent a brief moment composing his thoughts, while the tension of this already awkward situation mounted unbearably.

7 Remember, he said eventually, catching both brothers completely unaware, People are the same the world over; no one is what they seem.

8 Never trust anyone.

9 Everyone is your enemy until they have proved themselves your friend, and even then never give them the benefit of the doubt.

10 Avoid those with whom you are unfamiliar. Walk in the shadows. Be alert. Carry weapons. Speak to no one unless you are spoken to first, but still keep them at arm's length.

11 Distance is your salvation.

12 Guard yourself against acts of treachery and deceit: for they will be about you always.

13 As Amos had expected, Voles was not listening – or, at least, he did not appear to be listening: for he had adopted his usual condescending attitude towards Amos that only suggested that his father was incapable of telling him anything worth hearing. Voles just shrugged his shoulders, scuffed his feet and muttered

something unintelligible under his breath (which was about as good a response as any these days). Yet Amos remained hopeful.

14 However, of these things never spoken before the good son then asked, But father, if we do as you say, how will we know the truth about anyone?

15 Amos then turned to Yule and replied sagely, You will know what they are by the things you hear them say about other people.

16 But what if -

17 Enough! cried Amos, and with that, and armed with this knowledge more valuable to their cause than any material possession, Yule and Voles waved goodbye to their father (who, incidentally, had two fingers crossed behind his back at the time), ventured forth into the world and were never heard of again.

‘To the Special Friends of Alison Coombs-Dunbar’

Lucy recognised Amy from some way off. She was below the promenade where it bends towards the pier, sitting alone and probably thinking big thoughts – or perhaps about nothing at all.

Amy hadn’t changed a bit. She was exactly the same as Lucy remembered: bare feet, faded blue play pants (ripped at the knees and seat), a red and white striped T-shirt, and a mane of orange curls. Lucy couldn’t imagine Amy any other way. She always looked the same, and Lucy usually knew where to find her. Sometimes she just had to think about Amy and she’d turn up, and at other times Amy couldn’t be further from her mind when suddenly she’d appear quite unexpectedly. Either way, Lucy was always pleased to see her friend.

Over a week had gone by since they’d last met properly, and after that Lucy’s mum had said maybe they should steer clear of each other for a while and perhaps Lucy should think about making some new friends instead. Lucy knew both Mummy and Ms Matthews from school thought Amy was a bad influence and they’d all be much happier if Lucy didn’t see her any more. But of course, as best friends know, that just wasn’t possible.

Lucy wriggled carefully through the lines of

holidaymakers who streamed by in search of even more amusements to fill the day until tea, now that the novelty of the resort had worn thin – along with the contents of Dad's pockets and Mum's purse. She stopped for a moment by the railings and gazed down to where a tiny fragile figure sat against the massive concrete wall. Amy never thought about the strange behaviour of summer tourists. For her, the promising award of 'UNLIMITED NUDGES', or the immediate delight of three 'Bars' in a row, could just as easily be found in the thin ribbon of things that ran down the length of the beach, or in the power of a wave, crashing at your feet, that thumped you in the breast like a football. Amy couldn't understand why anyone would want to spend the whole afternoon swinging the limp claw of a pretend crane over a lot of stale chocolates, when you could plunge your hand into a rock pool and haul out a fistful of shellfish whenever you felt hungry.

Amy knows the beach as well as anyone. She knows all the living things that crawl about or swim or fly around in the air. She knows pebbles and shells. She knows the stuff that gets washed ashore and what it can be used for as well. She knows how the beach works. She watches how the action of the sea wears away the lime cliffs and draws sand from the estuary. She knows clouds and rain. She knows the tides and the moon. She knows the seasons. She knows the length of a year. She knows the sun, how it rises and shines before it sets, and she knows the night sky. She knows herself and what it means to be alive. She knows love. She knows the world. She knows the past and the present...

Lucy climbed down the steps to the beach, but instead of leaping off the last and burying her feet in the sand as normal, she walked cautiously along the base of the wall towards her friend, leaning outwards to be more conspicuous.

Amy, however, in apprehension more than spite, kept her eyes narrowed and focused on some distant point of amazement lying just beyond the horizon. She always sat like that when she was unhappy. It was something to do with the sea air, how it dried your skin, put your teeth on edge and made your hair all frizzy. There was nothing else like it. Amy could withstand the heat and spray and sand in her face forever, when anyone else would just turn away.

She'd told Lucy about it. Lucy didn't really understand but she knew it was important to Amy, so they just sat together in silence, as old friends do, and stared out across the ocean towards some far off imaginary shore.

They both knew they would talk eventually. They would be united and go on again as before, a little older and a bit wiser, but for the moment there was a lot to think about.

Lucy put her hand around her wrist, as Amy had shown her, and found she was again and more than ever before out of time with the pulse of the sea. The tears swelled in her eyes, and when she raised her head they streamed down her face to leave two great stains on her white school blouse. She was adrift. A part of nothing. Pretend. A fake. She didn't belong anywhere and in trying she'd lost so much of herself, or buried or denied the very things about her Amy loved. She'd even denied Amy. She'd told the others Amy wasn't her friend any more, which was just as well because she wouldn't be allowed at the party if she was. Amy was stupid and childish, and if Lucy wanted a slice of Alison's birthday cake she'd better hurry up and say that out loud. Lucy did say it out loud. She repeated it, just to make sure, and then said it out loud again, as she laughed wildly and crawled about on the carpet with her mouth full of sponge cake and jam.

They'd all been so delighted when she'd received the invitation. Lucy was becoming quite the little socialite. But why shouldn't she be invited? Wasn't she exactly the same as everyone else? Perhaps it was a mistake or another cruel joke like the last time. Well, surely a simple phone call would straighten that out.

Daddy nodded approvingly when he put down the receiver; the invite was genuine enough.

To the Special Friends of Alison Coombs-Dunbar the hand-delivered envelope had said, and inside Lucy's name in bold print somewhere in the middle of a lavishly illuminated pink and gold card. The details were less interesting, except for the date, which was next Saturday and gave Mummy practically no time at all to organise an outfit and find a present.

The excitement lasted all week and was perfectly understandable, but there was nothing whatever to be surprised about. Lucy was simply going to the birthday party of Alison Coombs-Dunbar, but for some strange reason everyone seemed to find that difficult to believe. The woman behind the Italian counter in Tesco was quite astonished when she was told, and Simone from the dry-cleaner's was practically speechless.

Sometimes Mummy got angry with people. At others there were tears in her eyes, but Lucy never really knew why. She often felt different in the company of other children; the reaction of adults towards her was just as confusing, and although she saw her reflection in a pool the same as any other, mirrors always disturbed her. Janet Osborn and Teresa Robbins had held her down and pushed one in her face shortly before she'd ran off down the road crying and spent the entire night on the dunes with Amy, which was a very stupid thing to do, even though it was the middle of summer and the nights were short and mild.

Somehow she always ended up with Amy. Amy was her excuse for everything!

Lucy began to think about why she'd deserted Amy and remembered the last time she'd abandoned her friend – and the awful lines, curves and dots that still puzzled her.

Ms Matthews brought them out last term and they'd played around with them for the rest of the afternoon until the beeper went and it was time to leave for the Christmas holidays. Lucy helped gather them all up and put them back in the box and thought, like the big jigsaw or squeezy clay that everyone got bored with, Ms Matthews wouldn't bother with them again and there would be something much more fun to play with when they got back. In the meantime, they should all practice their wiggles and shapes – that was important.

Ms Matthews drew wiggles and shapes on the floppy board and everyone copied down what she'd drawn. Lucy coloured in her wiggles and shapes and even made up some of her own and coloured them in too, to please Ms Matthews even more. Wiggles and shapes is a much better game than lines, curves and dots, but all the time now, for ages and ages until going home time, everyone plays lines, curves and dots, and no one plays wiggles and shapes any more except Lucy.

It wasn't her fault, but she should have waited all the same.

She'd ran out of school clutching her wiggles and shapes and was miles away by the time she remembered Rodger Pemberton, Emma's dad, was picking them both up today because Daddy's van was buggered and he couldn't make it as usual. By the time she got back, the school gates were locked and there was no one around to ask.

She set off on her own again, and somehow, God only knows, she crossed the big road beside the park that led up to Emma's, but all the houses looked different from the back and she couldn't see enough over the high wooden fences.

It was getting dark and she heard voices from the shelter and got scared. She climbed through a space beside a hedge and into a garden she didn't know. There was no one home and no way through to the front, so she sat on a bench by the fishpond and watched the rain slashing all around her, on the surface of the water and on the wiggles and shapes.

Well, she must have fallen asleep or passed out or something, and could quite easily have fallen in and drowned if Mrs Kowalski hadn't forgotten her purse for the bingo, or if the cat stayed out in all weathers, or if that useless lump of a husband of hers wasn't sat in front of the telly all day, and the poor little lamb was handed over to the search party sent out to rescue her, and everyone agreed she'd been a very lucky girl. Honestly, anything could have happened – and you do hear so many terrible stories these days!

Lucy remembered being cold and wet and carried into the house, where Daddy was shouting down the phone at Rodger Pemberton about sewing him a shirt for his back and Mummy, who always thought the worst in everything, was saying she would never have forgiven herself if... what she couldn't bring herself to say... Still, what a relief it was to have her back in one piece safe and sound.

Then she was standing by the fire and getting out of all those wet things that Mummy didn't know what to do with, and they all tried to think what in heavens had gotten into her, and 'No! No! No!' she told the wobbly-pea-sea, she hadn't spoken to anyone.

Later, she was in bed and Dr Nadiar was making faces and telling Mummy he was sure there was nothing to worry about but it might be best to keep her indoors for the next few days, which meant the trip to Nan's was out the window – again! But the hospital was much better than Nan's, and Mummy and Daddy, and Rodger and Joyce Pemberton, and Emma, and even Mrs Kowalski came to visit, and every time they did they always brought something they shouldn't, and after Kevin in the next bed, who anyone could see she'd been fond of, had gone away to his very own special place in the sky, there were still lots of other children to play with, but when there weren't she could always play wiggles and shapes by herself whenever she wanted.

It was funny going back to school again after all that time and some of it she didn't remember. Ms Matthews said Mummy wasn't to worry about a thing; they would all look after her, and Emma promised to keep a close eye on her throughout the day.

Lucy fell asleep in the morning and had a little bit of an accident and got all upset when they couldn't get anyone on the phone. But by the afternoon everything was back to normal and there was nothing whatever to worry about, and everyone played lines, curves and dots, and when Ms Matthews asked to see everyone's lines, curves and dots Lucy showed Ms Matthews her wiggles and shapes, all perfectly coloured in with special new felt pens for being such a brave girl from Uncle Joe.

And still Lucy sat looking at the lines, curves and dots she'd been given because it was ages since then and now she was no different from anyone else. They were lots of blue and pink cards that made noises and when you put them together they had names, and the names were put together to tell stories. Emma knew all about lines, curves and dots. She'd shown Lucy to start with but was already telling stories, and Mummy said she shouldn't be held back helping Lucy because that was Ms Matthews' job – it's what she got paid for!

But Ms Matthews had shown Lucy. She'd shown her time and time again, but she had to think of the rest of the class. Mummy and Daddy had shown her as well and couldn't think where they'd gone wrong, and even Tom Dulcie, who called himself a head teacher and was something of an expert in fields, had tried and done everything he could for her, and what's more there was absolutely no point in crying about it or feeling sorry for herself, she couldn't play lines, curves and dots and that was all there was to it.

What on earth were they going to do? They couldn't go on like this, that was for sure. For God's sake, something would have to be done! But they were all at their wits' end already.

Lucy looked at the cards again spread out on the table in front of her. They were everywhere now, on the classroom walls, in the street, on everything in shops and even at home where she'd never seen them before – lines, curves and dots that you thought were wiggles and shapes until you looked closely and they'd suddenly jump out at you but wouldn't make a sound.

She knew most of them were sideways on or upside down because that was just typical, but they were square and you couldn't tell.

Ms Matthews wasn't watching. Anyone could see she was concentrating on someone else.

Lucy picked up the cards and counted them out into two piles of blue and pink. There were twenty-one blue and five pink – twenty-six in all. The same number of felt pens Uncle Joe had given her – it said so on the pack: *26*. Lucy thought for a moment: 26. That's thirteen times two, or four times six and a half, or three hundred and sixty-four divided by fourteen, or the sum of...

But that wasn't how you played lines, curves and dots.

Lucy dried her eyes and thought again about what could have driven her away from Amy. On both occasions, at the end of the autumn term and when she learnt about the party, Lucy remembered being in some strange other world she knew was unreal but very pleasant and safe. She didn't understand the others, or all the funny ways they shared that brought them together, but she did at least recognise in herself a very deep and longing desire to be exactly the same. The more she behaved like them the less frightening they became, and although she might eventually be allowed in their company Amy would never be accepted. It was like a game, but a game like no other. A game in which everyone else knew the rules except you and no one was telling.

Lucy took a deep breath and held it in for as long as she could before breathing out heavily, as though expelling something horrid from her body. She still couldn't bring herself to look at Amy, but knowing Amy was listening and would wait forever to hear what she had to say eased the delivery of her confession.

'I told a lie when I said I had other friends. I don't have other friends.'

There was a short pause before Lucy turned to Amy, but Amy didn't move or say a word. There was no need.

'Do you have other friends?' Lucy asked warily.

Again Amy said nothing but just screwed her bottom lip and turned her head a little to one side before resuming her stationary pose.

And that was that. Lucy and Amy sat together for the rest of the afternoon, mostly in silence but with occasional exchange, and as the sun fell into the sea before them, gradually they were reunited.

Lucy thinks about Amy and how different she is from her but how alike. No one ever notices Amy. She is never singled out or pointed at in the street. No one ever laughs or stares at her, and no one ever calls her names. Lucy doesn't know why the others won't make friends with Amy because Amy will make friends with anyone who cares to know her.

Amy is not like the others but something else that is difficult to explain. She is something disturbing, something wonderful. Something unusual to be drawn towards, not because you think you should but because you know you want to. She is something through and beyond that which is familiar and comfortable and might take a bit of time to get to know – like the odd little girl sitting talking to herself on the sea wall.